PHP MYSQL

Programming

Real World Code

2 Books in 1

For Beginners

Ray Yao

About the Authors: Ray Yao's Team

Certified PHP engineer by Zend, USA

Certified JAVA programmer by Sun, USA

Certified SCWCD developer by Oracle, USA

Certified A+ professional by CompTIA, USA

Certified ASP. NET expert by Microsoft, USA

Certified MCP professional by Microsoft, USA

Certified TECHNOLOGY specialist by Microsoft, USA

Certified NETWORK+ professional by CompTIA, USA

www.amazon.com/author/ray-yao

About This Book

Total length of this book is 328 pages, it includes two parts:

1. PHP MYSQL Programming for Beginners

2. PHP MYSQL Real World Code & Explanations.

Part 1:

"PHP MYSQL Programming" is a textbook for high school and college students; it covers all essential PHP MYSQL language knowledge. You can learn complete primary skills of PHP MYSQL programming fast and easily.

The textbook includes a lot of practical examples for beginners and includes exercises for the college final exam, the engineer certification exam, and the job interview exam.

Part 2:

"PHP MYSQL Real World Code" includes a lot of PHP MYSQL practical examples & explanations for beginners.

Through these useful examples & explanations, you can study PHP MYSQL programming skills in depth, master skillfully the PHP MYSQL coding knowledge, and become an expert of PHP MYSQL programming.

These examples & explanations cover various types of PHP MYSQL programming skills, such as operators, statement, array, string, function, class, object, file processing, exception......, which can be applied to the real PHP MYSQL programming work.

Table of Contents

Part One

Programming

for Beginners

Chapter 1

What is PHP?

PHP is a server-side language for web development, meaning "Personal Homepage Program".

PHP is a scripting language executed on the server, especially for Web development and embedded in HTML.

PHP supports both object-oriented and procedural development and is very flexible to use.

PHP is free and widely used, making PHP an effective language.

PHP can generate dynamic page content.

PHP can create, open, read, write, and close files on the server.

PHP can collect form data to the server.

PHP can send and receive cookies.

PHP can add, delete and modify data in MySQL database.

PHP can restrict user to access some pages on our site.

PHP can encrypt data.

PHP can output image, pdf files and flash movies.

PHP can provide extensive database support.

Install PHP & MySQL

If we want to run PHP and MySQL, we need to set up the **development environment** on our own computer. Therefore we can install "AppServ" to set up a server.

AppServ

"**AppServ**" is free software to setup a server; it can run Apache, PHP, MySQL, PhpMyAdmin, Ajax, JavaScript, JQuery and Html file......, the link to download the AppServ is:

http://www.appservnetwork.com/

Please install AppServ to the folder "**C:\AppServ**".

The installer will install PHP first, and then install MySQL.

The parameters to install MySQL are:

MySQL default username: **root**

Please set a password: **12345678**

After installing AppServ, please **restart** the computer.

Restart & Test

Please restart computer, open a browser, and type a url address:

http://localhost

We can see the page like this: (The look may be different!)

The AppServ Open Project - 2.5.10 for Windows

phpMyAdmin Database Manager Version 2.10.3
PHP Information Version 5.2.6

About AppServ Version 2.5.10 for Windows
AppServ is a merging open source software installer package for Windows includes :

- Apache Web Server Version 2.2.8
- PHP Script Language Version 5.2.6
- MySQL Database Version 5.0.51b
- phpMyAdmin Database Manager Version 2.10.3

- ChangeLog
- README
- AUTHORS
- COPYING
- **Official Site** : http://www.AppServNetwork.com
- **Hosting support by** : http://www.AppServHosting.com

Change Language :

Easy way to build Webserver, Database Server with AppServ :-)

Congratulation! The installation is fully successful! PHP, MySQL and Apache server are running successfully!

Working Folder

Note: The folder "**C:\AppServ\www**" is a working folder of PHP programs. We can create one or more subfolders under the working folder, and put all our PHP program files to this working folder or its subfolders. From now on, we are able to run PHP files in "**C:\AppServ\www**" folder or its subfolders.

Hello World Program

The syntax of PHP looks like this:

```
<?php    ......    ?>
```

<?php ...... ?> means that all PHP codes are in here.

Example 1.1

Please open a Notepad, input PHP codes as follows:

```
<html>
<?php
echo ("Hello World!");
?>
</html>
```

Save the file with the file name "**hello.php**" to the **working folder.** (C:\AppServ\www").

Run the program by a browser with a URL as follows:

http://localhost/hello.php

Output:

Hello World!

Congratulation! The first PHP program runs successfully!

The syntax of PHP code looks like this: <?php ...... ?>

<?php ...... ?> means that all PHP codes are in here.

"echo" is command of PHP, means "output" or "print".

"echo ("Hello World")" outputs "Hello World".

Each PHP statement must end with ";".

Note:

If you use a Notepad to write any other PHP programs, please

save it as "**xxx.php**" to the working folder (C:\AppServ\www),

then open a browser, and type a url address as follows:

---

http://localhost/xxx.php

The above url can run any "**xxx.php**" programs on a browser.

Comments

Comment is used to explain the code, make it understandable.

// symbol is used in single-line comments.

/*......*/ symbols are used in multi-line comments.

The PHP compiler always ignores all PHP comments.

Example 1.2

```php
<?php
echo (" OK ");    // output OK.
echo (" Hello ");    /* echo ("Hello"); is a PHP output command,
"echo" is a PHP reserved word, it shows or prints the word
"Hello" in here.  PHP is very easy to learn. */
?>
```

Output:

OK   Hello

Explanation:

<u>// output OK;</u> is a single-line comment.

<u>/* ...... */</u> is a multi-line comment.

The PHP compiler always ignores all PHP comments.

PHP Reserved Words

Some words are only used by PHP language itself. They cannot work as an identifier names for variable, function, and labels.

The following words are part of PHP reserved words:

and	array( )	break
case	const	continue
default	do	echo( )
else	else if	empty( )
eval( )	exception	exit( )
extends	false	for
function	foreach	global
if	include( )	include_once( )
isset( )	list( )	new
null	or	print( )
require( )	require_once( )	return( )
static	switch	true
unset( )	xor	while

Preserved words are also known as Keywords.

For Example:

---

if // "if" is a reserved word.

else // "else" is a reserved word.

Example 1.3

```php
<?php
$number = 1;
if (0 < $number ) {    // "if" is a reserved word.
echo "The number is positive";
}
else {    // "else" is a reserved word.
echo "The number is negative";
}
?>
```

Output:

The number is negative

Explanation:

In this program, **"if"** and **"else"** is the reserved words of PHP.

Note: Reserved words cannot work as the name of variable, constant, string, function, and array.

Variables

A variable is a container to temporarily store a value.

Variable name starts with "**$**" symbol.

The syntax to declare a variable is:

$variable

Example 1.4

```php
<?php

$var;      //declare a variable

$abcde;    // declare a variable

$my_variable;   // declare a variable

?>
```

Explanation:

A variable can store a specified value. For example:

$var = 100;   // $var has the value 100

$abcde = "Hello";   // $abcde has the value "Hello"

$my_variable = true;   // $my_variable has the value "true"

Note that variable name cannot start with a number, variable name cannot have spaces. e.g. "$23var", "$abc de" are invalid variable names. But "$var23", "$abcde" are valid variable names.

Data Types

The chief data types of PHP are:

String – characters within double or single quotation.

Integer – numbers without decimal point.

Boolean – a value with true or false.

Float – numbers with decimal point.

Example 1.5

```
$str='I am a string';

$int=168;

$float=12.88;

$bool=true;
```

Explanation:

$str='I am a string';   // data type is String.

$int=168;   // data type is Integer.

$float=12.88;   // data type is Float.

$bool=true;   // data type is Boolean.

Note: String is always enclosed by a pair of double quotes or single quotes. e.g. "abcde", 'learning'.

Escaping Characters

The " \ " backslash character can be used to escape characters.

Escape	Description
\n	outputs content to the next new line.
\r	makes a return
\t	makes a tab
\'	outputs a single quotation mark.
\"	outputs a double quotation mark.

Example 1.6

```php
<?php

echo "PHP said \" Hello World \" ";

// the \" can output a double quotation mark.

?>
```

Output: PHP said "Hello World"

Explanation:

 \" outputs a double quotation mark.

Another sample: echo "Hello \t\t\t World";   // three tabs

// Output: Hello   World

Functions

A function is a code block that can be repeatedly run many times.

1. The syntax to define a function is:

---

function function-name ( ) {......}

---

2. The syntax to call a function is:

---

function-name ( );

Example 1.7

```php
<?php
function test( ){    // declare a function
echo ("This is a function example.");   // output
}
test( );    // call the function
?>
```

Output: This is a function example.

Explanation:

"function test( ){ }" defines a PHP function.

"test( );" calls the function named test( ){ }.

After the function test( ){ } is called , it will output "This is a function example.".

Function with Arguments

Arguments are used to pass data to function body.

1. The syntax to define a function with argument is:

function function-name ($argument){......}

2. The syntax to call a function with argument is:

function-name (parameter);

Example 1.8

```php
<?php
function test( $arg ){    // declare a function with arguments
echo ("$arg");
}
test("A function example");   // call the function, and pass args.
?>
```

Output: A function example

Explanation: When test("A function example") calls the function test($arg){...}, it passes the "A function example" to $arg. After $arg has received the parameter, it passes the parameter to the function body and outputs the parameter value.

Variable Scope

A global variable is declared **outside** the function, it can be used in everywhere; A local variable is declared **inside** the function, it is only used inside current function.

Example 1.9

```php
<?php

$num=200;      // this $num is a global variable.

function test( ){

$num=100;      // this $num is a local variable.

}

echo $num;

?>
```

Output:

200

Explanation:

"echo $num" outputs 200, which means that $num stores a value of global variable.

If we want to declare a global variable inside a function, we should use a keyword **"global"** preceding the variable name.

e.g. function test( ) { **global** $num; ......}

Multiple Arguments

A function may have several arguments; these arguments will pass data simultaneously to the function body.

The syntax to define a function with multiple arguments is:

function function-name ($arg1, $arg2, $arg3){......}

Example 1.10

```php
<?php

function test ($a, $b, $c){    // with multiple arguments

$sum=$a+$b+$c;    // calculation

echo $sum;    // output

}

 test(3, 6, 9);    // call the function, and pass parameters

?>
```

Output:

18

Explanation:

When test(3, 6, 9) calls the function test ($a, $b, $c){...}, the parameters 3,6,9 passes to the $a, $b, $c, and then passes the parameters to function body.

Hands-on Project: Calculation

Function Demo

Open the Notepad, input following codes to it:

```php
<?php

function multiply($x, $y){    // define a function with args

calculate($x, $y);    // call "calculate()", pass parameters

}

function calculate($a, $b){    // define a function with args

$result = $a * $b;    // calculate

echo("The value is $result");    // output the result

}

?>

<?php

multiply(10,20);    // call "multiply()", pass parameters 10, 20

?>
```

"Save" the file with a name "functionDemo.php", and run the
program by the url: http://localhost/functionDemo.php.

The value is 200

"function multiply($x, $y){… }" defines a function "multiply()".

"function calculate($a, $b){… }" defines a function "calculate()".

"multiply(10,20);" calls the function "function multiply($x, $y){… }", and passes two parameters 10, 20 to $x and $y.

"calculate($x, $y);" calls the function "function calculate($a, $b){…}", and passes two parameters 10, 20 to $a and $b.

If you use Notepad to create an above PHP program, please save it as **"functionDemo.php"** to the working folder (C:\AppServ\www), then run a browser, and type a following url address:

http://localhost/functionDemo.php

The above url can run "functionDemo.php" programs.

If you want to edit the "functionDemo.php" with Notepad, please right click the file > Open with > Notepad.

Chapter 2

Conditional Operator

The syntax of the conditional operator is as follows:

(test-expression) **?** (if-true-do-this) **:** (if-false-do-this);

Conditional operator checks if the test-expression is true or false, then, according to true or false to execute the specified block.

Example 2.1

```php
<?php
$a = 100;
$b = 200;
$result1 = ($a<$b) ? "apple " : "banana ";
// If ($a<$b) returns true, the result is "apple". Otherwise, the result is "banana"
echo ("$result1<br>");
$result2 = ($a>$b) ? "apple " : "banana ";
// If ($a>$b) returns true, the result is "apple". Otherwise, the result is "banana"
echo ("$result2<br>");
?>
```

apple

banana

Explanation:

The conditional operator uses ($a<$b) to test the $a and $b, because $a is less than $b, it returns true. Therefore, the output is "apple".

The conditional operator uses ($a>$b) to test the $a and $b, because $a is less than $b, it returns false. Therefore, the output is "banana".

Note:

The difference between "<br>" and "\n" is:

```
echo ("$variable <br> ");   // is used in html web page
```

"<br>" is used in HTML web page, run by a browser to output the content to the next new line.

```
echo ("$variable \n ");    // is used in php source code
```

"\n" is used in PHP source code, run by an editor to output the content to the next new line.

An informal method:)   After trying the <br>, if you are not satisfied with the output effect, please use "\n", and vice versa.

Arithmetical Operators

The arithmetic operators are as follows:

Operators	Running
+	add
-	subtract
*	multiply
/	divide
%	get modulus
++	increase 1
- -	decrease 1
.	connect two strings

Example 2.2

```php
<?php
$add = 100 + 200;    echo ("$add<br>");
$div = 800 / 2;    echo ("$div<br>");
$mod = 10 % 3;    echo ("$mod<br>");    // get remainder
$inc = 10;    echo (++$inc."<br>");        // increase 1
$str = "abc"."de";    echo ("$str<br>");    // connect two strings
?>
```

Output:

300

400

1

11

abcde

Explanation:

$add=100+200;   echo $add;   // output 300

$div=800/2;   echo $div;   // output 400;

$mod=10%3;   echo $mod;   // output 1;

$inc=10;   echo ++$inc;   // output 11;

$str="abc"."de"; echo $str;   // output abcde.

Logical Operators

The logical operators are as follows:

Operators	Same As
&&	and
||	or
!	not

The result of the logical operators will be true or false.

Example 2.3

```php
<?php
$a = true; $b = false;
$test1 = ( $a && $b ) ? "true " : "false ";     // and
$test2 = ( $a || $b ) ? "true " : "false ";     // or
$test3 = ( !$a ) ? "true " : "false ";     // not
$test4 = ( !$b ) ? "true " : "false ";     // not
echo ("$test1<br>");
echo ("$test2<br>");
echo ("$test3<br>");
echo ("$test4<br>");
?>
```

Output:

false

true

false

true

Explanation:

true && true;	true && false;	false &&false;
returns true;	returns false;	returns false;
true II true;	true II false;	false II false;
returns true;	returns true;	return false;
! false;	! true;	
returns true;	returns false;	

Assignment Operators

The assignment operators are as follows:

Operators	Examples	Same As
+=	$x+=$y	$x=$x+$y
-=	$x-=$y	$x=$x-$y
*=	$x*=$y	$x=$x*$y
/=	$x/=$y	$x=$x/$y
%=	$x%=$y	$x=$x%$y
.=	$x.=$y	$x=$x.$y

Example 2.4

```php
<?php
$x1 = $x2 = $x3 = $x4 = $x5 =200;
$y1 = $y2 = $y3 = $y4 = $y5 =100;
$x1 += $y1;  echo ("$x1<br>");    // x1=x1+y1
$x2 -= $y2;  echo ("$x2<br>");    // x2=x2-y2
$x3 *= $y3;  echo ("$x3<br>");    // x3=x3*y3
$x4 /= $y4;  echo ("$x4<br>");    // x4=x4/y4
$x5 %= $y5;  echo ("$x5<br>");    // x5=x5%y5
$m = "abc"; $n = "de";
$m .= $n;  echo $m;    // $m=$m.$n
?>
```

Output:

300

100

20000

2

0

abcde

Explanation:

$x+=$y;   // $x=$x+$y;

$x-=$y;   // $x=$x-$y;

$x/=$y;   // $x=$x/$y;

$x*=$y;   // $x=$x*$y;

$x%=$y;   // $x=$x%$y;

$m.=$n;   // $m=$m.$n;

Comparison Operators

The comparison operators are as follows:

Operators	Running
>	greater than
<	less than
>=	greater than or equal
<=	less than or equal
==	equal
!=	not equal

The result of the comparison operators will be true or false.

Example 2.5

```php
<?php
$a=100; $b=200;
$result1 = ($a>$b)? "true":"false";     // check if $a > $b
$result2 = ($a==$b)? "true":"false";    // check if $a == $b
$result3 = ($a!=$b)? "true":"false";    // check if $a != $b
echo ("$result1<br>");
echo ("$result2<br>");
echo ("$result3<br>");
?>
```

Output:

false

false

true

Explanation:

$result1 = ($a>$b);   // if 100>200; outputs false.

$result2 = ($a==$b);   // if 100==200; outputs false.

$result 3= ($a!=$b);   // if 100!=200; outputs true.

Review:

echo ("$result
"):   "<br>" is used in web page, run by a browser to output the content to the next new line.

echo ("$result\n"):   "\n" is used in source code, run by an editor to output the content to the next new line.

If Statement

The syntax of If statement is:

```
if ( condition ) {   // if true do this;   }
```

"if statement" executes codes inside { ... } only if the condition returns true, does not execute any codes inside {...} if the condition returns false.

Example 2.6

```php
<?php
$x = 200;
$y = 100;
if ( $x > $y ){    // if true, run following code
echo "x is greater than y.";
}
?>
```

Output:

x is greater than y.

Explanation:

($x>$y) is a test expression, namely (200>100), if it returns true, the codes inside the { } will be executed, if it returns false, the codes inside the { } will not be executed.

If/else Statement

The syntax of If/else statement is:

```
if ( condition ) {  // if true do this;  }
else  { // if false do this;  }
```

"if...else statement" executes the { // if true do this } if the condition returns true, otherwise executes the { // if false do this } if the condition returns false.

Example 2.7

```php
<?php
$x = 100; $y = 200;
if ( $x > $y ){   // if true, run this code block
echo "x is greater than y.";
}
else {   // if false, run this code block
echo "x is less than y";
}
?>
```

Output: x is less than y.

Explanation:

($x>$y) is a test expression, namely (100>200). If it returns true, the code will output "x is greater than y." If it returns false, the code will output "x is less than y".

Switch Statement

```
switch ( $variable ) {
case 1:  // if equals this case, do this;  break;
case 2:  // if equals this case, do this;  break;
case 3:  // if equals this case, do this;  break;
default :  // if not equals any case, run default code;  break;
}
```

The value of $variable will compare each case first, if it equals one of the "case" value; that "case" code will be executed.

If the $variable doesn't match any case, the "default" statement will be executed.

"break;" terminates the code running of the switch statement.

Example 2.8

```
<?php
$number = 20;
switch ( $number ) {   // $number will compare each case
case 10 : echo "Running case 10";  break;
case 20 : echo "Running case 20";  break;   // match this
case 30 : echo "Running case 30";  break;
default :  echo "Running default code";  break; }
?>
```

Running case 20

The $number value is 20; it matches case 20, so the code in case 20 is executed.

Note: the "break" command cannot be omitted, otherwise, an error will occur!

Example 2.9

```php
<?php
$number = 100;    // Note: the $number value is 100
switch ( $number ) {   // $number will compare each case
case 10 : echo "Running case 10";  break;
case 20 : echo "Running case 20";  break;    // match this
case 30 : echo "Running case 30";  break;
default :  echo "Running default code";  break;  }
?>
```

Running default code

Because $number=100, it does not match any case value, the "default" command is executed.

For Loop

"for loop" runs a block of code by the specified number of times.

The syntax of "for loop" is as follows:

```
for( init, test-expression, increment) { // some code; }
```

"init" initializes a variable that is used to control the loop.

"test-expression" allows looping if it returns true.

"increment" will increase 1 in every loop.

Example 2.10

```php
<?php
for ($x = 0; $x <= 5; $x++) {   // loop at most 5 times
echo "$x ";
}
?>
```

Output: 012345

Explanation:

$x = 0 initializes the value of $x,

$x <= 5 will specify that the "for loop" will run at most 5 times.

$x++ means that x will increase 1 in each loop.

After 5 times loop, the code will output 012345.

While Loop

The syntax of "while loop" is as follows:

```
while ( test-expression ) { // some php code in here; }
```

"while loop" loops through a block of code if the specified condition is true.

Example 2.11

```php
<?php
$counter=0;
while ($counter < 8){   // loop 8 times
echo "&";
$counter++;   // increase 1 in every loop
}
?>
```

Output: &&&&&&&&

Explanation:

"$counter< 8" is a test expression, if the condition is true, the "while loop" will run 8 times, until the $counter value is 8, then the condition is false, the "while loop" will stop running.

Do-While Loop

The syntax of do/while loop is as follows:

```
do{ // some php code in here } while ( test-expression);
```

"do...while" loops through a block of code once, and then repeats the loop if the specified condition is true.

Example 2.12

```php
<?php
$counter=0;
do {
echo "@";
$counter++;     // increase 1 in every loop
} while ($counter<8);   // loop 8 times
?>
```

Output:

@@@@@@@@

Explanation:

"$counter< 8" is a test expression, if the condition is true, the "do/while loop" will run 8 times, until the $counter is 8, then the condition is false, the "do/while loop" will stop running.

Break Statement

"break" keyword is used to stop the running of a loop according to the condition.

```
Break;
```

Example 2.13

```php
<?php
$num=0;
while ($num<10){
if ($num==5) break;   // exit the current loop if $num is 5
$num++;
}
echo ( $num );
?>
```

Output:

5

Explanation:

"if ($num==5) break;" is a break statement. If $num is 5, the program will run the "break" command, and exits the while loop, then run the next command "echo ($num)".

Continue Statement

"continue" keyword is used to stop the current iteration, ignores the subsequent code, and then continues the next loop.

```
continue;
```

Example 2.14

```php
<?php
$num=0;
while ($num<10){
$num++;
if ($num==5) continue;     // go to the next loop if $num is 5
echo ( $num );   // skip echo($num) if $num is 5
}
?>
```

Output:

1234678910

Explanation:

Note that the output has no 5.

About "if ($num==5) continue;", when the $num is 5, the program will run "continue", skips the next command "echo ($num)", and then continues the next loop.

Return Statement

"return value" is used to return a value to the function caller.

The syntax to return a value is:

```
return value;
```

Example 2.15

```php
<?php
function multiply($x, $y){
return $x * $y;    // return the value to the function caller
}    // the value of "$x*$y" is 200
?>
<?php
$result = multiply(10, 20);    // this is a function caller
echo $result;
?>
```

Output:

200

Explanation:

"return $x * $y;" returns a value "200" to "multiply(10, 20)". We can treat it as "multiply(10, 20) = 200".

Hands-on Project: One to Ten

Loop Statement Demo

Open your favorite PHP editor, input following codes to it:

```php
<?php
echo "while statement: <br>";
$value1 = 1;
while($value1<=10){    // loop at most 10 times
echo $value1." ";
$value1++;
}
echo "<br><br>";


echo "do...while statement: <br>";
$value2 = 1;
do{
echo $value2." ";
$value2++;
}while($value2<=10);   // loop at most 10 times
echo "<br><br>";


echo "for statement: <br>";
```

```
for($i=1;$i<=10;$i++){   // loop at most 10 times

$value3 = $i;

echo $value3." ";

}

?>
```

"Save" the file with name **"loopDemo.php"**, and run the program.

Output:

while statement:
1 2 3 4 5 6 7 8 9 10

do...while statement:
1 2 3 4 5 6 7 8 9 10

for statement:
1 2 3 4 5 6 7 8 9 10

Explanation:

"while loop" loops through a block of code if the specified

condition is true.

"$value1< =10" is a test expression, if the condition is true, the

code will loop 10 times,

"do...while" loops through a block of code once, and then repeats

the loop if the specified condition is true.

"$value2< =10" is a test expression, if the condition is true, the code will loop 10 times,

"for($i=1;$i<=10;$i++)" runs a block of code according to the specified number of times.

"$i = 1" initializes the variable "i" as 1.

"$i<=10" sets the loop's number of times.

"$i++" increases 1 in each loop.

Chapter 3

Create an Array

An array is a particular variable, which can contain one or more value in the meantime.

array( ) is used to create an array.

(1) The first syntax to create an array is:

```
$arrayName = array ("value0", "value1", "value2");
```

(2) The second syntax to create an array is:

```
$arrayName = array ( );

$arrayName[index0] = "value0";

$arrayName[index1] = "value1";

$arrayName[index2] = "value2";
```

Example 3.1

```php
<?php

$color = array ( );        // create an array $color

$color [0] = 'red';        // initialize the array element

$color [1] = 'yellow';     // initialize the array element

$color [2] = 'green';      // initialize the array element
```

```
echo "$color[0]<br>";

echo "$color[1]<br>";

echo "$color[2]<br>";

?>
```

Output:

red

yellow

green

Explanation:

Above code creates an array, array name is $color, it has three elements: $color [0], $color [1], $color [2]. Its indexes are 0, 1, and 2. Its values are red, yellow, and green.

Array index begins counting from zero.

array element values

The syntax to get the value of an array element is:

```
$arrayName[index]
```

Example 3.2

```php
<?php

$color = array("yellow", "purple", "orange");

// create an array

echo ( $color[1] );

// show the element value at the index 1

?>
```

Output:

purple

Explanation:

The value of $color[0] is yellow.

The value of $color[1] is purple.

The value of $color[2] is orange.

Note that array index begins counting from zero.

Get the Size of Array

Two syntaxes to get the size of an array are as follows:

count($array);
sizeof($array);

Example 3.3

```php
<?php
$color = array("yellow", "purple", "orange");
$size1= count($color);    // get the size of the array
$size2 = sizeof($color);    // get the size of the array
echo ( "$size1  " );
echo ( "$size2  " );
?>
```

Output:

3   3

Explanation:

"count($color)" or "sizeof($color)" can return the size of the array $color. array("yellow", "purple", "orange") has three elements, so its size is 3.

Array keys & Values

Array elements can consist of key / value pairs, the syntax is:

array(key1=>value1, key2=>value2, kay3=>value3...);

"=>" symbol is used to connect key and value.

(key and index is the same meaning in Array.)

Example 3.4

```php
<?php
$book=array( "A"=>"JSP", "B"=>"ASP", "C"=>"PHP");
// "A" is a key, "JSP" is a value
// "B" is a key, "ASP" is a value
// "C" is a key, "PHP" is a value
echo $book[ "C" ];   // show the element value at the key "C"
?>
```

Output:

PHP

Explanation:

A character can work as an index of the array.

"echo $book[C]" shows the value of $book[C].

Iterate Array

foreach() can iterate over all elements of an array, the syntax is:

```
foreach( $array as $key=>$value ){ }
```

Each array key is assigned to $key, each array value is assigned to $value, until it iterates the last array element.

Example 3.5

```php
<?php
$book=array( "A"=>"JSP", "B"=>"ASP", "C"=>"PHP");
foreach ( $book as $key => $value ){   // iteration
echo "The $key  book is about  $value. <br>";
}
?>
```

Output:

The A book is about JSP.

The B book is about ASP.

The C book is about PHP.

Explanation:

"foreach ($book as $key=>$value)" assigns $book's key to $key, assigns $book's value to $value in each loop iteration. In the first loop iteration, "A" is assigned to $key, "JSP" is assigned to $value, and so on......

Add Array Elements

We can add an element to the beginning of an array, or add an element to the end of an array.

1. array_unshift(array, value1, value2) adds value1, value2 to the beginning of the array.

The syntax of array_ unshift() is:

```
array_unshift( array, value1, value2...);
```

2. array_push(array, value1, value2...) adds value1, value2 to the end of the array.

The syntax of array_push() is:

```
array_push( array, value1, value2... );
```

Example 3.6

```php
<?php
$myArray=array("A", "B", "C");
array_unshift($myArray, "START");
// add "START" to the beginning of the array
array_push($myArray, "END");
// add "END" to the end of the array
```

```
echo ( "$myArray[0] " );      // show "START"

echo ( "$myArray[1] " );

echo ( "$myArray[2] " );

echo ( "$myArray[3] " );

echo ( "$myArray[4] ");       // show "END"

?>
```

Output:

START A B C END

Explanation:

array_unshift($myArray, "START") adds the element "START" to the beginning of the $myArray.

array_push($myArray, "END") adds the element "END" to the end of the $myArray.

There are five elements in $myArray now.

Remove Array Elements

We can remove an element from the beginning of an array, or remove an element from the end of an array.

1. array_shift (array) removes an element from the beginning of the array.

The syntax of array_shift() is:

```
array_shift( array );
```

2. array_pop (array) removes an element from the end of the array.

The syntax of array_pop() is:

```
array_pop( array);
```

Example 3.7

```php
<?php
$myArray=array("START", "A",  "B", "C", "END");

array_shift($myArray);   // remove the first element

array_pop($myArray);     // remove the last element

echo ( "$myArray[0]  " );

echo ( "$myArray[1]  " );

echo ( "$myArray[2]  " );

?>
```

Output:

A B C

Explanation:

array_shift($myArray) removes the first element in the $myArray.

array_pop($myArray) removes the last element in the $myArray.

There are only three elements in $myArray now.

Merge Array

array_merge(array1, array2) can merge array1 and array2, and returns a new array.

The syntax of array_merge() **is:**

```
array_merge( array1, array2 );
```

Example 3.8

```php
<?php
$array1=array ("A", "B", "C");
$array2=array ("D", "E", "F");
$array=array_merge( $array1, $array2 );   // merge arrays
foreach( $array as $value) { echo("$value " );}
?>
```

Output:

A B C D E F

Explanation:

array_merge($array1, $arra2) can merge two arrays to a new array $array. After two arrays has been merged, the new array has six elements; therefore, the program returns ABCDEF.

Extract Array

array_slice(array, start, length) can extract some elements from an array according the specified start index and length, returns a new array. The syntax of array_slice() is:

array_slice(array, start, length);

"start" specifies the start point to extract array elements.

"length" specifies the length to extract array elements.

Example 3.9

```php
<?php
$array=array("A","B","C","D","E","F");
$arr=array_slice( $array, 2, 3 );
// extract three elements from index 2
foreach($arr as $value){ echo "$value ";}
?>
```

Output:

C D E

Explanation:

array_slice(array, 2, 3) extracts 3 elements from the index 2 of the $array.

Sort Array

sort(array) can sort the array elements values in alphabetical order.

The syntax of sort() is:

```
sort ( array );
```

Example 3.10

```php
<?php
$color =array("yellow", "red", "blue", "white");
sort ( $color );   // sort the elements in alphabetical order
foreach( $color as $value ) { echo "$value ";}
?>
```

Output:

blue red white yellow

Explanation:

sort ($color) rearranges the sequence of the $color elements values in alphabetical order. After all element values have been sorted, the program outputs a new element values sequence "blue red white yellow".

Hands-on Project: Start with Zero

Iterate Array Demo

Open your favorite PHP editor, input following codes to it:

```php
<?PHP

$a = array("zero", "one", "two");

echo "In array('zero', 'one', 'two'): <br><br>";

foreach ($a as $key => $v){

// store element keys to $key, store element values to $v

echo "About the element in the index ".$key." : <br>";

echo "The key is: ".$key.",   ";

echo "The value is: ".$v. "<br><br>";

}
?>
```

Save the file with name **"arrayDemo.php"**, and run the program.

In array('zero', 'one', 'two'):

About the element in the index 0 :

The key is: 0, The value is: zero

About the element in the index 1 :

The key is: 1, The value is: one

About the element in the index 2 :

The key is: 2, The value is: two

"$a = array("zero", "one", "two");" creates an array named $a.

"foreach ($a as $key => $v)" assigns array $a's key to $key, assign array $a's value to $value in each loop iteration. In the first loop iteration, "0" is assigned to $key, "zero" is assigned to $value, and so on......

Chapter 4

Create a Form

Html form is used to submit data to the server, and let the PHP process the data.

Example 4.1

```
<form  action= "PHP MySQL.php"  method="get" >

......

<form>
```

Explanation:

action= "PHP MySQL.php" specifies a PHP file named "PHP MySQL.php" to process the data from this HTML form.

action= " " specifies the current PHP file to process the data from this HTML form.

If the Form has no "action=...", then the current PHP file will process the data from the HTML form by default.

For example:

action = "myfile.php", it specifies a PHP file named "myfile.php" to process the data from the HTML form.

"method="get"" specifies "get" method to send data to the server, the data is open, all users can view the passing data.

"method="post"" specifies "post" method to send data to the server, the data is hidden, no users can view the passing data.

Text Inputs

```
<input type="text"  name="data">
```

input type="text" specifies the input type as "text",

name="data" specifies the inputted "data" that will be passed to the PHP file for processing.

Example 4.2

```
<form action=" "  method="get">
<input type="text"  name="data">
</form>
```

Display:

```
[                    ]
```

Explanation:

action= " " specifies the current PHP file to process the data from this HTML form.

"method="get"" specifies "get" method to send data to the server, the data is open, all users can view the passing data.

input type="text" specifies the input type as "text",

name="data" specifies the inputted "data" that will be passed to the PHP file for processing.

Password Inputs

input type="password" name="data"

input type="password" specifies the input type as "password",

name="data" specifies the inputted "data" that will be passed to the PHP file for processing.

Example 4.3

```
<form action="  "  method="post">
<input type="password"  name="data">
</form>
```

Display:

Explanation:

action= " " specifies the current PHP file to process the data from this HTML form.

"method="post"" specifies "post" method to send data to the server, the data is hidden, no users can view the passing data.

input type="password" specifies the input type as "password".

name="data" specifies the inputted "data" that will be passed to the PHP file for processing.

Submit Input

The syntax to submit input is:

```
<input type="submit"  value="characters">
```

type="submit" specifies to submit all data in the form to the server.

value="characters" specifies the characters shown on a button.

Example 4.4

```
<form action="myfile.php"  method="post">

<input type="submit"  value="Submit">

</form>
```

Display:

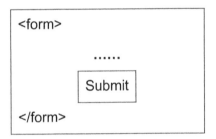

Explanation:

action = "myfile.php" specifies a PHP file named "myfile.php" to process the data from the HTML form.

type="submit" specifies to submit all data in the form to the server.

value="Submit" specifies the "Submit" shown on a button.

Reset Inputs

The syntax to reset input is:

```
<input type="reset"  value="characters">
```

type="reset" specifies to reset all data in the form.

value="characters" specifies the characters shown on a button.

Example 4.5

```
<form action="myfile.php"  method="post">
<input type="reset"  value="Reset">
</form>
```

Display:

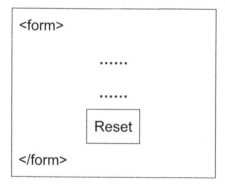

Explanation:

type="reset" specifies to reset all data in the form.

value="Reset" specifies the "Reset" shown on a button.

Textarea Inputs

The syntax of textarea is:

```
<textarea  name="data"  rows="num"  cols="num">
```

"<textarea>" type specifies the input type as "textarea".

name="data" specifies the inputted "data" that will be passed to the PHP file for processing.

rows="num" specifics the number of rows in the text area.

cols="mum" specifics the number of columns in the text area.

Example 4.6

```
<form action="myfile.php"  method="post">

<textarea  name="data"  rows="5"  cols="10">

</form>
```

Display:

Explanation: name="data" specifies the inputted "data" that will be passed to the PHP file for processing.

rows="5" specifies the number of rows as 5.

cols="10" specifies the number of columns as 10.

Radio Inputs

The syntax of radio inputs is:

```
<input type="radio"  name="data"  value="content">
```

type="radio" specifies to input data by single choice.

name="data" specifies the inputted data that will be passed to the PHP file for processing.

value="content" specifies one of the contents that will be selected.

Example 4.7

```
<input type="radio"  name="color" value="red">

<input type="radio"  name="color" value="blue">

<input type="radio"  name="color" value="pink">
```

Display:

○ red   ○ blue   ○ pink

Explanation:

type="radio" allows us select one of the circles.

name="color" specifies the selected data "color" that will be passed to the PHP file for processing.

value="red" specifies one of the selected values as "red".

Checkbox Inputs

The syntax of checkbox inputs is:

```
<input type="checkbox"  name="data"  value="content">
```

type="checkbox" specifies to input data by multiple choice.

name="data" specifies the inputted data that will be passed to the PHP file for processing.

value="content" specifies one of the contents that will be selected.

Example 4.8

```
<input type="checkbox"  name="color" value="red">

<input type="checkbox"  name="color" value="blue">

<input type="checkbox"  name="color" value="pink">
```

Display:

☐ red   ☐ blue   ☐ pink

Explanation:

type="checkbox" specifies to input data by multiple choices.

name="color" specifies the selected data "color" that will be passed to the PHP file for processing.

value="red" specifies one of the selected values as "red".

Form Works with PHP (1)

The syntax to get data from the HTML form is:

```
$_GET[ data ];      // get data from html form
```

Example 4.9

```
<html>

<body>

<form action=" "  method="get">

<input type="text"  name="data">

<!-- the inputted value will be stored to the "data" -->

<!--"data" will be passed to the PHP file for processing. -->

</form>

<?php

$myData = $_GET[ data ];

// $_GET[ data ] gets the "data" value from the html form

echo ("You have inputted: ".$myData);  // show data value

?>

</body>

</html>
```

Save the file with the name **"getFile.php"** in the working folder, and run it by a browser: http://localhost/getFile.php

(Assume that you input "Hello" and enter.)

Output:

```
Hello
```

You have inputted: Hello

Explanation:

action=" " specifies the current PHP file to process the data coming from the HTML form.

method="get" specifies "get" method to send data to the server, the data is open, all users can view the passing data.

(method="post" specifies "post" method to send data to the server, the data is hidden, no users can view the passing data.)

name="data" stores the inputted value to "data", and passes the data value to the PHP file for processing.

$_GET[data] gets the data from html form.

$myData = $_GET[data] gets the value of "data" from the html form, and assign the value to $myData.

Form Works with PHP (2)

The syntax to receive data from the HTML form is:

```
$_POST[ data ];    // receive data from the html form
```

Example 4.10

```
<html>

<body>

<form action=" "  method="post">

<input type="text"  name="data">

<!-- the inputted value will be stored to the "data" -->

<!--"data" will be passed to the PHP file for processing. -->

</form>

<?php

$myData = $_POST[ data ];

// $_POST[ data ] receives the "data" value from the html form

echo ("You have inputted: ".$myData);   // show data value

?>

</body>

</html>
```

Save the file with the name **"postFile.php"** in the working folder, and run it by a browser: http://localhost/postFile.php

(Assume that you input "Hello" and enter.)

Output:

```
Hello
```

```
You have inputted: Hello
```

Explanation:

action=" " specifies the current PHP file to process the data coming from the HTML form.

method="post" specifies "post" method to send data to the server, the data is hidden, no users can view the passing data.

(method="get" specifies "get" method to send data to the server, the data is open, all users can view the passing data.)

name="data" stores the inputted value to "data", and passes the data value to the PHP file for processing.

$_POST[data] receives the data value from html form. The data value is "Hello".

$myData = $_POST[data] receives the value of "data" from the html form, and assign the value "Hello" to $myData.

Hands-on Project: Radio's Colors

Radio Demo

Open your favorite PHP editor, input following codes to it:

```
<html>

<p>Please Select Your Favorite Color</p>

<form method = get >

<!-- user input by radio button -->

<input type="radio" name="color" value="Red" >Red<br>

<input type="radio" name="color" value="Yellow" >Yellow<br>

<input type="radio" name="color" value="Green" >Green<br>

<br>  <!-- the "color" value will pass to PHP to process -->

<input type="submit" value="Submit"> <br>  <!-- submit -->

</form>

</html>

<?php

echo "You Selected:  ";

$hobby = $_GET['color'];   // get the "color" value

echo($hobby);

?>
```

Save the file with name **"radioDemo.php"** in the working folder, and run the program: http://localhost/radioDemo.php

(Assume that we select "Green", and Submit.)

Output:

Please Select Your Favorite Color

○ Red
○ Yellow
◉ Green

[Submit]

You Selected: Green

Explanation:

method="get" specifies "get" method to send data to the server, the data is open, all users can view the passing data.

name="color" stores the inputted value to "color", and passes the color value to the PHP for processing.

$_GET[color] gets the value of "color" from the html, the value is "Green".

$hobby = $_GET[color] gets the value of "color" from the html form, and assign the value "Green" to $hobby.

Chapter 5

Date & Time

The syntax to show the date and time is:

```
date("M  d  Y");
date( "h : i : s");
date("D  H  A");
```

date("M d Y") displays month, date, year.

date("h : i : s") displays hour, minutes, second.

date("D H A") displays Day, Hour, AM/PM

Example 5.1

```php
<?php
$date = date("M  d  Y ");
$hour = date( "h : i : s ");
$week = date("D  H  A ");
echo $date;
echo $hour;
echo $week;
?>
```

Output: Nov 26 2015 02 : 29 : 02 Thu 14 PM

Explanation:

Format	Description	Example
a	'am' or 'pm' lowercase	pm
A	'AM' or 'PM' uppercase	PM
d	Day of month, a number with leading zeroes	18
D	Day of week (three letters)	Thu
F	Month name	January
h	Hour (12-hour format - leading zeroes)	11
H	Hour (24-hour format - leading zeroes)	23
g	Hour (12-hour format - no leading zeroes)	11
G	Hour (24-hour format - no leading zeroes)	23
i	Minutes (0 - 59)	23
j	Day of the month (no leading zeroes	18
l	Day of the week	Monday
L	Leap year ('1' for yes, '0' for no)	1
m	Month of year (number - leading zeroes)	1
M	Month of year (three letters)	May
n	Month of year (number - no leading zeroes)	3
s	Seconds of hour	18
U	Time stamp	968292368
y	Year (two digits)	08
Y	Year (four digits)	2006
z	Day of year (0 - 365)	206
Z	Time Zone from GMT	+5

String Functions

The syntax of the string functions is:

```
strlen( );      // return a length of a string

strtoupper( );     // return an uppercase string

strtolower( );     // returns a lowercase string
```

Example 5.2

```php
<?php
$string=" Hello World!  ";
echo strlen( $string );    // return string length
echo strtoupper($string);    // return uppercase
echo strtolower($string);    // return lowercase
?>
```

Output:

16   HELLO WORLD! hello world!

Explanation:

strlen($string) returns 16.   (The length includes whitespaces.)

strtoupper($string) returns HELLO WORLD!

strtolower($string) returns hello world!

Redirection of Browser

The header () in PHP is used to redirect the user from one page to another page. The syntax of header() is:

```
header( "Location : $url");
```

header("Location : $url") can redirect the user from one page to another page.

"$url" specifies where to go.

Example 5.3

```php
<?php

header( "Location:http://www.amazon.com");   // redirection

?>

<html>

<body>

......

</body>

</html>
```

Explanation:

"header("Location:http://www.amazon.com") ;" redirects the user to www.amazon.com.

Visitor Browser Information

The syntax to get the information about the visitor's browser is:

```
$_SERVER["HTTP_USER_AGENT"];
```

$_SERVER ["HTTP_USER_AGENT"] returns the information about the browser of a visitor.

Example 5.4

```
<?php
$browser = $_SERVER["HTTP_USER_AGENT"];
echo "$browser";
?>
<html>
......
</html>
```

Output:

Mozilla/4.0 (compatible; MSIE 8.0)...

Explanation:

$_SERVER["HTTP_USER_AGENT"] returns the visitor's browser information.

Cookie

The syntaxes to set or get a cookie value are as follows:

```
setcookie ( "name",  "value" );   // set cookie name and value

$_COOKIE["name"];    // get cookie value by cookie name
```

A cookie is usually used to identify a user. It is a way to store a user's information across multiple pages.

The cookie contains the cookie "name" and cookie "value".

Usually we can set a cookie in the a.php file, and get the cookie in the b.php file.

Example 5.5

1. a.php

```
<?php   // in a.php

setcookie("color", "blue");    // set a cookie name and value

// cookie name is "color", cookie value is "blue"

header("location: b.php");     // redirect to b.php

?>
```

Save this file with the name "**a.php**" in the working folder, but do not run the "a.php" in this moment.

2. b.php

```php
<?php  // in b.php

$myColor = $_COOKIE["color"];   // get the cookie value

// get the cookie value whose name is "color" from "a.php:

echo  $myColor;   // show the value of $myColor

?>
```

Save the file with the name **"b.php"** in the working folder.

Please run the "a.php" (http://localhost/a.php)

Output:

blue

Explanation:

In a.php, setcookie("color", "blue") sets a cookie name as "color" and value as "blue".

In b.php, $_COOKIE["color"] gets the cookie value whose name is "color", and the value is "blue" from a.php.

In the example, we can know:

The cookie name and cookie value of the a.php can be passed to b.php.

Session

The session is usually used to identify a user. It is a way to store information across multiple pages in a website.

The "session id" is used to track each visitor and correlate data across the multi-webpage.

SID is a unique session id, a 32 hexadecimal random number.

The syntax to start a session is:

```
session_start()
```

The syntax to pass the session id to another page is:

```
<a href = "anotherPage.php  <?php echo(SID);?>">...</a>
```

Example 5.6

1. A.php

```
<?php session_start()?>   <!-- start php session -->

Here is "First Page".<br><br>

Send out a session id to the second page<br><br>

<a href = "B.php<?php echo(SID);?>">To Second Page </a>
<!-- pass session id to the B.php -->
```

Save this file with the name **"A.php"** in the working folder, but do not run the "A.php" in this moment.

The syntax to get the session id is:

```
session_id()
```

"session_id()" gets the session id from the related page.

2. B.php

```
<?php session_start()?>   <!-- start php session -->

Here is "Second Page".<br><br>

The session id is: <br><br>

<?php echo(session_id());?>   <!-- show session id -->
```

Save the file with the name "**B.php**" in the working folder.

Please run the A.php (http://localhost/A.php)

Output:

Here is "First Page".

Send out a session id to the second page

To Second Page

(Please click the above link "To Second Page".)

Output:

Here is "Second Page".
The session id is:
m4tiga6576moc23dma5jugt8cm

Explanation:

<?php echo(**SID**);?> contains a session ID, which makes data available across the multiple pages in a whole website.

SID is a unique session id, a 32 hexadecimal random number.

"session_start()" starts a session.

"session_id()" gets the session id from the related page.

If we click the "To Second Page", the session id in the A.php will be passed to the B.php.

In the example, we can know:

The session name and session value of the A.php can be passed to B.php.

Session Usage

The syntaxes to set and get a session name, session value are:

```
$_SESSION["name"]=value;    // set session name & value
$_SESSION["name"];      // get session value by name
```

Example 5.7

1. a.php

```php
<?php session_start( );
$_SESSION ["color"] = "green";    // set color as green
header("location: b.php");
?>
```

2. b.php

```php
<?php session_start( );
$carColor = $_SESSION ["color"];   // get the value of color
echo $carColor;
?>     <!-- Please run the a.php -->
```

Output: green

Explanation:

In a.php, "$_SESSION["color"] = "green"" sets a session name as color and value as green.

In b.php, $_SESSION ["color"] gets the session value whose name is "color", and the value is "green" from a.php.

Open a File

The syntax to open a file is:

```
fopen ($fileObj, mode);
```

The mode to open a file is:

Mode	Operation
r	open file for reading only, read from the beginning.
w	open file for writing only, clear original content.
a	open file for writing only, append new content.
x	create a new file for writing only.

Note: If above modes with "**+**" sign, means opening the file for reading and writing. e.g. r+, w+, a+, x+

Example 5.8

```
$fileObj = "myfile.txt";

fopen( $fileObj, r );     // open the file for reading only

fopen( $fileObj, w );     // open the file for writing only
```

Explanation:

"fopen($fileObj, r)" opens the myfile.txt for reading. "fopen($fileObj, w)" opens the myfile.txt for writing.

Write a File

The syntax to write a file is:

```
fwrite( $openfile, "content");
```

"fwrite( )" writes the contents to a file.

"$openfile" specifies the opened file to write.

"content" specifies the content to write.

Example 5.9

```php
<?php
$fileObj = "D:\myfile.txt";   // set the path D:\myfile.txt
$openfile = fopen( $fileObj, w );   // open a file with w mode
fwrite( $openfile, "PHP is very good!" );   // write
echo "Write a file successfully! Please  check myfile.txt.";
?>
```

Output:

Write a file successfully! Please check myfile.txt.

Explanation: (If you open the D:**myfile.txt**, you can see the contents "PHP is very good!").

"fwrite($openfile, "PHP is very good!")" writes the content "PHP is very good!" to the myfile.txt file.

Read a File

The syntax to read a file is:

```
fread( $openfile, length );
```

"fread()" reads the content of a file.

"$openfile" specifies the opened file to read.

"length" specifies the maximum number of bytes to read.

Example 5.10

// Assume that the content of myfile.txt: "PHP is very good!"

// The path of the myfile.txt is: D:\myfile.txt

```php
<?php
$fileObj = "D:\myfile.txt";
$openfile = fopen( $fileObj, r );    // open a file with r mode
$content = fread( $openfile, 20 );    // read 20 bytes
echo "$content";
?>
```

Output:

PHP is very good!

Explanation:

"fread($openfile, 20)" reads 20 bytes from myfile.txt, and reads it from the beginning.

Close a File

The syntax to close a file is:

```
fclose($openfile);
```

"$openfile" specifies the file that has been opened.

It is good practice to close the opened file after using that. We can release the memory resource, and other processes that may be still used by the file.

Example 5.11

```php
<?php
$fileObj = "D:\myfile.txt";    // set the path D:\myfile.txt
$openfile = fopen( $fileObj, w );   // open a file with w mode
fclose($openfile);     // close the opening file
 ?>
```

Output:

This page isn't working

Explanation:

After opening the myfile.txt, we can use fclose($openfile) to close the opened file.

Hands-on Project: Extraction.

substr( ) Demo

The syntax to extract a substring from a string is:

```
substr(string, start, length)
```

substr(string, start, length) extracts a substring by the specified parameters.

"string" specifies a string to extract a substring.

"start" specifies the start position to extract the substring.

"length" specifies the length to extract the substring.

Open your favorite PHP editor, input following codes to it:

```php
<?php
echo 'substr("JavaScript in 8 Hours!",4,6) returns: '."<br>";
echo substr("JavaScript in 8 Hours!",4,6)."<br><br>";
echo 'substr("JavaScript in 8 Hours!",11) returns: '."<br>";
echo substr("JavaScript in 8 Hours!",11)."<br><br>";
?>
```

Save the file with name "**substrDemo.php**", and run the program.

by the url: http://localhost/substrDemo.php.

103

substr("JavaScript in 8 Hours!",4,6) returns:

Script

substr("JavaScript in 8 Hours!",11) returns:

in 8 Hours!

Explanation:

substr("JavaScript in 8 Hours!",4,6)." extracts a substring from the original string "JavaScript in 8 Hours", starts from index 4, the length of substring is 6 characters.

substr("JavaScript in 8 Hours!",11)." extracts a substring from the original string "JavaScript in 8 Hours", starts from index 11, the length of the substring is from index 11 to the end.

Chapter 6

Class

Class is a category with the same feature and property, class is a template for an object.

The syntax to define a class is as follows:

```
class ClassName{    // define a class

var $variable;    // define a variable

function functionName ( ){ }    // define a function

}
```

The variable is also known as "property" in the class.

The function is also known as "method" in the class.

Example 6.1

```
class Flower {    // define a class "Flower"

var c1; var c2;    // declare two variable c1 and c2

function beautify() {...}    // declare a method beautify()

}
```

Explanation:

"class Flower" defines a class named "Flower".

"var c1; var c2;" defines two variables named "c1" and "c2".

"function beautify()" defines a method named "beautify()".

Object

Object is an instance of a class.

An object can reference a variable or a method.

The syntax to create an object is as follows:

```
$object = new ClassName;     // create a new object

$object->variable;     // $object references a variable

$object->functionName( );     // $object references a function
```

Note: The "variable" has no "$" symbol in" $object->variable;".

Example 6.2

```
$obj = new Flower;

$obj->c;

$obj->beautify();
```

Explanation:

"$obj = new Flower;" creates an object named" $obj".

"$obj->c" means that $obj references variable "c".

"$obj->beautify();" means that "$obj" references the method beautify( ){...}.

Note: in" $obj->c;", the "c" has no "$" symbol.

Class & Object

Example:

```php
<?php
class Flower{     // define a class
var $c = "Beautiful\n";     // define a variable $c
function beautify(){     // define a function beautify()
echo ("The flower is beautiful" );
}}
$obj= new Flower();     // create an object $obj
echo $obj -> c;     // $obj references "c"
$obj -> beautify();     // $obj references beautify()
?>
```

Output:

Beautiful

The flower is beautiful

Explanation:

"class Flower" defines a class "Flower".

"$obj= new Flower();" creates an object "obj".

$this -> variable

$this represents the current object. The syntax is:

$this -> variable;   // $this references a variable

Note that a variable has no "$".

Example 6.3

```php
<?php
class Flower{      // define a class "Flower"
var $c = "Flower is beautiful";
function beautify() {
echo $this -> c;      // $this represents $obj
}}
$obj= new Flower();      // create an object $obj
$obj -> beautify();      // $obj references the beautify(){ }
?>
```

Output: Flower is beautiful

Explanation:

"$this->c" means that the current object references the variable "c" in the current class. $this represents "$obj".

Note: in"$this->c", the "c" has no "$".

Constructor (1)

The constructor is used to initialize the class's variable. when an object is created, the constructor will be called automatically.

The constructor name is the same as the class name.

Example 6.4

```php
<?php
class Flower{    // define a class Flower
var $c;
function Flower( $arg ) {    // define a constructor
$this->c= $arg;     // initialize the variable c
echo $this->c;
}}
$obj= new Flower( 'Beautiful' );    // create an object $obj
?>
```

Output:

Beautiful

Explanation:

"function **Flower($arg){** $this->c= $arg; }" is a constructor.

When the object $obj is created, the constructor will be called automatically, and the argument "Beautiful" is sent to constructor.

Constructor (2)

"__construct( )" works as a constructor. The syntax is:

```
__construct( );    // is used to initialize class's variables
```

Example 6.5

```php
<?php
class Flower{    // define a class
var $c;
function __construct( $arg ) {    // constructor
$this->c= $arg;    // initialize the variable c
echo $this->c;
}}
$obj= new Flower( 'Beautiful' );    // create an object
?>
```

Output:

Beautiful

Explanation:

"function __construct ($arg) { }" defines a constructor.

When the object $obj is created, the constructor will be called automatically, and the argument "Beautiful" is sent to constructor.

Destructor

The destructor will be called when the object is destroyed or the program is stopped and exited. The syntax is:

```
__destructor( );   // destructor is used to release the resources
```

Example 6.6

```php
<?php
class Flower{
var $c;
function __construct( $arg ) {   // define a constructor
$this->c= $arg;   echo $this->c;
}
function __destruct( ) {    // define a destructor
echo " Destructor runs... ";
}}
$obj= new Flower( ' Constructor runs... ' );
?>
```

Output:

Constructor runs...   Destructor runs...

Explanation:

"function __destructor" defines a destructor, which can destroy the current object and release the resources.

Extend Class

When a child class extends a parent class, child class also inherits the variable and function from parent class.

The syntax for a child class to extend a parent class is:

```
class ChildClass extends ParentClass {......}
```

Example 6.7

```
class animal {

// define a parent class

}

class dog extends animal{    // extend

// define a child class

}

class monkey extends animal{    // extend

// define a child class

}
```

Explanation:

The class dog and the class monkey are two child classes, they extend their parent class "animal", also extends all features of the parent class.

Extending Example

The child class can inherit all features of the parent class.

The object of child class can reference the variable and function of the parent class.

Example 6.8

```php
<?php
class Animal{     // define a parent class
var $head;     // parent class's variable
function tail( ) {     // parent class's function
echo "Dog's tail is small";
}}
class Dog extends Animal{
 // child class extends parent class
}
$d = new Dog( );     // create an object of the child class
$d->head = "big"; // reference the variable of the parent class
echo "Dog's head is ".$d->head."<br>";
$d->tail( );     // reference the function of the parent class
?>
```

Dog's head is big

Dog's tail is small

$d is an object of the child class.

"$d->head" references the variable of the parent class.

"$d->tail( );" references the function of the parent class.

Class::method ( )

Usually an object can call a method, but in PHP a class can also call a method by using :: symbol.

A class can use :: to call a method directly.

The syntax of a class calling a method is:

```
Class :: method( );
```

Example 6.9

```php
<?php
class A {
function display( ) {
echo "Function A is called <br>";
```

```php
}

}

class B extends A {

function show() {

A :: display( );    // class A calls the method display(){ }

echo "Function B is called <br>";

}

}

B :: show( );    // class B calls the method show(){ }

?>
```

Output:

Function A is called

Function B is called

Explanation:

"A :: display( );" means that Class A calls display( ).

"B :: show( );" means that Class B calls show( ).

Hands-on Project: Appointment

Class & Object

Open your favorite PHP editor, input following codes to it:

```
<html>
<?php
class setDate{     // define a class "setDate"
var $day;      // declare three variable members
var $month;
var $year;
function __construct($m,$d,$y){     // constructor
$this->month=$m;      // initialization
$this->day=$d;
$this->year=$y;
echo "Constructor is called!<br><br>";
echo "The date is: ".$this->month."/".$this->day."/".$this->year;
echo "<br><br>";
}
function __destruct(){    // destructor
echo "Destructor is called!";
}
}
```

```
$obj=new setDate("12","6","2015");   /* create an object, and
call the constructor automatically */

?>

</html>
```

"Save" the file with the name "classobject.php" in the working folder, and run the program. (http://localhost/classobject.php)

Constructor is called!

The date is: 12/6/2015

Destructor is called!

Explanation:

"class setDate" creates a class "setDate".

"var $day; var $month; var $year;" defines three variable members.

function __construct($m,$d,$y){ ......} defines a constructor, which is used to initialize three variables.

"$this-> variable;" is used to access the variable in the current class. $this represents the current object.

"function __destruct()" defines a destructor, which is used to release resources.

The destructor will be called when the object is destroyed or the program is stopped and exited.

"$obj=new setDate("12","6","2015")" creates an object $obj, and automatically calls the constructor, and sends three parameters to the constructor for initializing variables.

The values of "$this->month; $this->day; $this->year;" are 12, 6 and 2015 respectively.

Chapter 7

What is MySQL?

MySQL is a database management system which is composed of one or more tables; the table arranges the data into organized rows and columns.

The row in the table is also known as "record".

The column in the table is also known as "field"

The table of database looks like this:

id	color1	color2	color3	color4	color5
1	red	yellow	green	blue	sky
2	pink	navy	purple	orange	olive

What does MySQL do?

MySQL Server is a database management system, which can add, access, modify, remove, and work with data stored in a computer database.

MySQL Data Type

The data types of MySQL are as follows:

Type	Explanation
int	An integer

decimal	A floating point number
date	A date in YYYY-MM-DD format
time	A time in HH:MM:SS format
year	A year in YYYY format
char( )	A string of defined fixed length
varchar( )	A string of defined changeable length
text	A string from 0 to 65535 characters

Example 7.1

When creating a database, we should declare the data type first.

The syntax to declare the data type is as follows:

```
id int,

color varchar(20)
```

Explanation:

"id **int**": the column name is "id", the data type is "int".

"color **varchar(20)**": The column name is "color", the data type is "varchar(20)", which is a string, its changeable length is 20.

Column Modifiers

The column modifiers of database are as follows:

Modifiers	Explanation
auto_increment	automatically increase in value
not null	must contain data
unique	must be only one of its kind
primary key(arg)	specifies its argument as primary key

Primary key is used to identify each record in a table uniquely.

Example 7.2

When creating a database, we should use the column modifiers.

The syntax to use column modifiers is as follows:

```
id int auto_increment,
color varchar(20) not null,
primary key(id)
```

Explanation:

"id int **auto_increment**": The value id can be automatically increased than the previous value.

"color varchar(20) **not null**": The data in "color" column cannot be empty.

"**primary key**(id)" specifies "id" as a primary key.

phpMyAdmin

The "phpMyAdmin" is popular software of the visual MySQL, many experienced programmers usually use phpMyAdmin to run MySQL. If you have installed "AppServ" to your computer, you can run **"phpMydmin"** to administrate the database.

Note: phpMyAdmin's appearance may be different in various versions, but they have the same usage.

Run "phpMyAdmin"

Please start up a browser, and enter an url as follows:

http://localhost/phpmyadmin

username: **root**,   password: **12345678**

You can see the page like this: (Maybe different!)

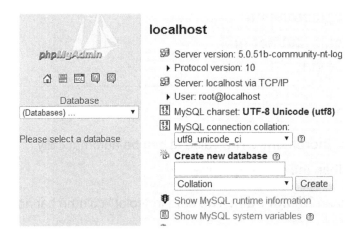

Show Databases

Show Databases

The syntax to display all existing database in the server is:

show databases;

Note: phpMyAdmin's appearance may be different in various versions, but the usage is the same.

Example 7.3

Please click the **"SQL"** tag in the Toolbar as following:

Or click the third button "SQL".

You can see a **"Run SQL query/queries window"** like this:

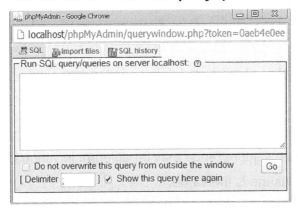

(The above window is called "Run SQL query/queries window",
which is usually used to enter MySQL commands)

Please enter commands:

show databases;

Then click the button "Go".

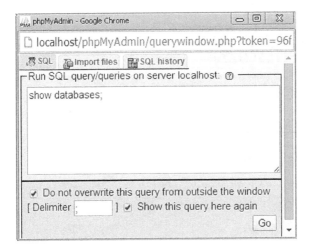

Output:

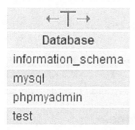

Explanation:

"show databases;" displays four existing databases in the server currently. They are "information_schema", "mysql", "phpmyadmin" and "test". (There are four databases in my computer server.)

Note:

When you want to use **"Run SQL query/queries window"** again to enter other MySQL commands, please click the **"SQL"** tag in the TaskBar.

Then you can click **"Edit"** to re-enter MySQL commands.

Create a Database

The syntax to create a new database is:

create database databaseName;

"databaseName" specifies a database name.

Example 7.4

Please click the **"SQL"** tag in the TaskBar as follows:

Open **"Run SQL query/queries window"** like this:

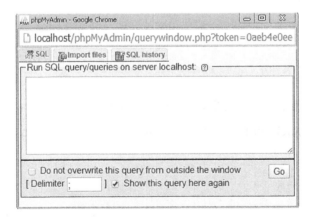

Please enter commands:

create database study;

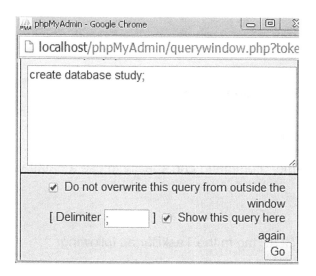

Output:

ⓘ Your SQL query has been executed successfully

┌ SQL query: ──────────────────────────────
│ CREATE DATABASE study

Explanation:

"create database study;" creates a database named "study".

You can click **"Edit"** to re-enter MySQL commands if necessary.

Select a Database

The syntax to select a database is:

```
use  databaseName;
```

"use databaseName" command can specify to use a database.

Example 7.5

Please click the **"SQL"** tag in the TaskBar as following:

Open **"Run SQL query/queries window"** like this:

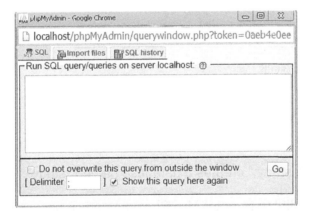

Please enter a command:

```
use study;
```

Click the button "Go".

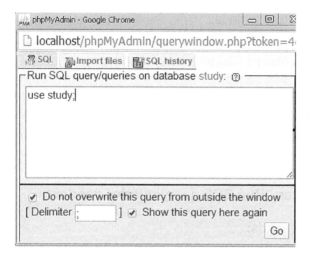

Output:

(i) Your SQL query has been executed successfully

SQL query:
USE study;

Explanation:

"use study;" specifies to use an existing database "study".

You can click **"Edit"** to re-enter MySQL commands if necessary.

Create a table

The syntax to create a table is:

create table tableName(column name data type,…);

"column name data type,…" specifies the table's column name and its data type.

Example 7.6

Click **"SQL"** to open **"Run SQL query/queries window.**

Please enter commands:

use study;

create table colortable(id int auto_increment, color1 varchar(20), color2 varchar(20), color3 varchar(20), primary key(id));

```
SQL    Import files    SQL history
Run SQL query/queries on server localhost: ⑦ -
use study;
create table colortable(id int auto_increment,
color1 varchar(20), color2 varchar(20), color3
varchar(20), primary key(id));
```

Click the button "Go".

Output:

ⓘ Your SQL query has been executed successfully

```
┌ SQL query: ─────────────────────────────
CREATE TABLE colortable(
    id INT AUTO_INCREMENT ,
    color1 VARCHAR( 20 ),
    color2 VARCHAR( 20 ),
    color3 VARCHAR( 20 ),
    PRIMARY KEY ( id )
);
```

Explanation:

"create table **colortable**" creates a table named "**colortable**".

"id int" specifies a column named "id", data type as "int".

"color1 varchar(20)" specifies a column named "color1", data type as "varchar(20)".

"id int auto_increment " specifies that the value of the "id" column will increase automatically.

"primary key(id)" specifies the "id" as primary key.

Primary key is used to identify each record in a table uniquely.

We can use primary key to select a record.

You can click **"Edit"** to re-enter MySQL commands if necessary.

Show Tables

The syntax to show all tables in the current database is:

```
show  tables;
```

Example 7.7

Click **"SQL"** to open **"Run SQL query/queries window"**.

Please enter commands:

```
use study;

show tables;
```

Click the button "Go".

Output:

Tables_in_study
colortable

Explanation:

"show tables;" shows the existing table "colortable" in database "study."

Insert Data to Table

The syntax to insert data to a table is:

> insert into tableName (column1, column 2, column3) values (value1, value2, value3);

"column1, column 2, column3" will be respectively inserted data by "value1, value2, value3"

Example 7.8

Click **"SQL"** to open **"Run SQL query/queries window"**.

Please enter commands:

> **use study;**
>
> **insert into colortable (color1, color2, color3) values ("red", "yellow", "green");**

Click the button "Go".

Output:

(To browse the table, please see next page.)

Explanation:

"color1, color 2, color3" will be respectively inserted data by "red, yellow, green".

Browse Table

The syntax to browse a table is:

```
select  *  from  tableName;
```

"select * from tableName;" can display a specified table.

"*" represents all columns in the table.

Example 7.9

Click **"SQL"** to open **"Run SQL query/queries window"**.

Please enter commands:

```
use study;

select * from colortable;
```

Click the button "Go".

Output:

colortable

id	color1	color2	color3
1	red	yellow	green

Explanation:

"select * from colortable;" shows all column data in "colortable"

Alter table & add column

The syntax to alter a table and add a column is:

```
alter  table  tableName  add columnName  type;
```

New column can be added to a table by using the "alter" command.

Example 7.10

Click **"SQL"** to open **"Run SQL query/queries window"**.

Please enter commands:

```
use study;

alter table colortable add color4 varchar(20);
```

Click the button "Go".

Please use following command to browser table.

```
use study;   select * from colortable;
```

Click the button "Go".

Output:

id	color1	color2	color3	color4
1	red	yellow	green	NULL

Explanation:

"add color4 varchar(20)" adds a new column named "color4".

Update...Set...

The syntax to update table & column value is:

```
update tableName set columnName=value where id=int;
```

A column value can be updated according to its id.

Example 7.11

Click **"SQL"** to open **"Run SQL query/queries window"**.

Please enter commands:

```
use study;

update colortable set color4="blue" where id=1;
```

Click the button "Go".

Please use following command to browser table.

```
use study;   select * from colortable;
```

Click the button "Go".

Output:

id	color1	color2	color3	color4
1	red	yellow	green	blue

Explanation:

"set color4="blue" where id=1" can update the value "null" to "blue" in the row where id is 1.

Select Query

The syntax of select query is:

```
select  columnName  from  tableName;
```

"select columnName from tableName" can show a specified column data in the table.

Example 7.12

Click **"SQL"** to open **"Run SQL query/queries window"**.

Please enter commands:

```
use study;

select color2 from colortable;
```

Click the button "Go".

Output:

color2
yellow

Explanation:

"select color2 from colortable" shows data of color2 from colortable.

Database Commands

MySQL Commands	Descriptions
CREATE DATABASE databaseName	create a database
USE databaseName	use a database
SHOW databaseName	show a database
DROP databaseName	remove a database

Table Commands

MySQL Commands	Descriptions
CREATE TABLE tableName	create a table
SHOW TABLES	show all tables
DESCRIBE	show a table property
DESC	show a table property
SHOW COLUMNS FROM tableName	show column property of a table
SHOW INDEX FROM tableName	show index property of a table
ALTER TABLE tableName	change table data
DROP TABLE tableName	remove a table
OPTIMIZE tableName	optimize a table

Field Modifiers

Modifier	Descriptions
AUTO_INCREMENT	automatically generate a serial number
NUT NULL	cannot be empty value
NULL	can be empty value
UNIQUE	cannot not duplicate any entry
PRIMARY KEY	specify a primary key
DEFAULT	specify a default value for a column
INDEX	find rows with specific column values

Operation Commands

Modifier	USE
SELECT column FROM table WHERE condition	query data
INSERT INTO table (column) VALUES (value)	insert data
DELETE FROM table WHERE condition	delete data
UPDATE table SET column = value WHERE condition	update data
REPLACE INTO table (column) VALUES (value)	replace data

Hands-on Project: Database

Create a database with a table

(1) Open phpMyAdmin. (http://localhost/phpMyAdmin)

(2) Enter username: **root**,   password: **12345678.**

(3) Click **"SQL"** to open **"Run SQL query/queries window"**,
   create a database named **"mydb"**, enter a command:
   create database mydb;

   Click the button **"Go"**.

(4) Click **"SQL"** to open **"Run SQL query/queries window"**,
   create a table named **"mytable"**, enter a command:
   use mydb;
   create table mytable(id int auto_increment, book1
   varchar(20), book2 varchar(20), book3 varchar(20),
   primary key(id));

   Click the button **"Go"**.

(5) Click **"SQL"** to open **"Run SQL query/queries window"**, insert data into the table "**mytable**", enter commands:

use mydb;

insert into mytable (book1, book2, book3) values ("PHP", "JSP", "ASP");

insert into mytable (book1, book2, book3) values ("LAMP", "J2EE", "HTLM");

Click the button **"Go"**.

(6) Click **"SQL"** to open **"Run SQL query/queries window"**, to browse the table, please enter:

use mydb;

select * from mytable;

Click the button **"Go"**.

(7) You can see a new database "**mydb**" with a table "**mytable**" as follows.

id	book1	book2	book3
1	PHP	JSP	ASP
2	LAMP	J2EE	HTML

143

Chapter 8

Require a File

The syntax to import another file to the current file is:

```
require( "myfile.php" )     // import myfile.php
```

"require()" is usually put in the beginning of the file.

Example 8.1

1. myfile.php

```
<?php   echo "I am from myfile.php<br>";  ?>
```

Save the file with the name **"myfile.php"** in the working folder.

2. ourfile.php

```
<?php

require("myfile.php");     // import myfile.php to here

echo "We are from ourfile.php<br>";

?>
```

Save the file with the name **"ourfile.php"** in the working folder.

Please run the ourfile.php (http://localhost/ourfile.php)

I am from myfile.php

We are from ourfile.php

"require("myfile.php")" imports myfile.php to the current file.

While the program uses require(), if the program has an error, a message will appear, but the program will stop.

Include a File

The syntax to import another file to the current file is:

```
include( "myfile.php" )    // import myfile.php
```

"include()" is usually put in the middle of the file.

Example 8.2

1. myfile.php

```php
<?php   echo "I am from myfile.php<br>";  ?>
```

Save the file with the name **"myfile.php"** in the working folder.

2. ourfile.php

```php
<?php
echo "We are from ourfile.php<br>";
include("myfile.php");   // import myfile.php to here
?>
```

Save the file with the name **"ourfile.php"** in the working folder.

Please run the ourfile.php (http://localhost/ourfile.php)

Output:

We are from ourfile.php

I am from myfile.php

Explanation:

"include("myfile.php")" imports myfile.php to the current file.

Note:

While the program uses include(), if the program has an error, a message will appear, but the program will keep running.

Connect MySql Server

The syntax to connect MySQL server is:

---

mysqli_connect("host", "username", "password");

"mysqli_connect( )" connects MySql server.

Return true if the connection is successful.

"host": specifies a host name.

"username": specifies a MySql username.

"password": specifies a MySql password.

Example 8.3

```php
<?php
$con= mysqli_connect( "localhost", "root", "12345678" );
if( $con ) {    // if connect MySQL server successfully
echo  " Connect successfully! ";
}
?>
```

Save this file with name "**connect.php**" to the working folder.

Please run this program by http://localhost/connect.php

Output:

Connect successfully!

Explanation:

"$con=mysqli_connect("localhost", "root", "12345678")" tries to connect MySql server. If successful, it returns true, if failed, it returns false.

"if ($con)" can check if the connection is successful or not.

We can use another syntax to connect a MySQL server:

```
new mysqli(host, username, password)
```

Example:

```php
<?php
$mysqli= new mysqli( "localhost", "root", "12345678" );
if( $mysqli ) {    // if connect MySQL server successfully
echo  " Connect successfully! ";
}
?>
```

Output:

Connect successfully!

Select Database

```
mysqli_select_db( $con, "databaseName" );
```

The mysqli_select_db( ) is used to select a database.

Return true if the selection is successful.

"$con" is the connection to MySql server. (See previous page).

"databaseName" specifies the name of the database.

Example 8.4

```php
<?php
require("connect.php");    // import "connect.php"
$select=mysqli_select_db( $con, "study" );
if( $select ) {   // if select database "study" successfully
echo  " Select db successfully!<br> ";
}
?>
```

Save this file with name **"select.php"** to the working folder.

Please run this program by http://localhost/select.php

Output:

Connect successfully! Select db successfully!

Explanation:

"require("connect.php");" imports "connect.php", the "connect.php" comes from previous several pages.

"$select=mysqli_select_db($con, "study");" tries to select a database "study". If successful it returns true. If failed it returns false. "study" is a database created previously.

"if ($select)" can check if the selection is true or false.

We can use another syntax to select a MySQL database:

```
$mysqli -> select_db(database_name)
```

Example:

```
$mysqli= new mysqli( "localhost", "root", "12345678" );

$mysqli -> select_db( "study" );    // select database "study"

if( $mysqli ) {    // if select database "study" successfully

echo  "Select database 'study' successfully!";

}
```

Output:

Select database 'study' successfully!

Insert Table Data

The syntax to insert data into a table is:

$sql="**insert into** tableName (columns) **values** (\"data\")";

$query=**mysqli_query**($con, $sql);

$sql="insert into tableName (columns) value (data)" is used to insert data into table.

$query=mysqli_query($con, $sql) executes the query.

"$con" is the connection to MySql server. (See previous page).

Note: In the PHP code, if we use MySQL command to insert strings into a table, the strings should be enclosed by \" symbols.

For example: ("\ string1 \", "\ string2 \", "\ string3 \").

Example 8.5

```php
<?php
require("select.php");    // import "select.php"
$sql="insert into colortable (color1, color2, color3, color4) values
(\"pink\",\"navy\",\"purple\",\"orange\")";
$query=mysqli_query( $con,$sql);  // execute query
if( $query ) {
echo  "Insert data successfully! ";
}
?>
```

Save this file with name **"insert.php"** to the working folder.

Please run this program by http://localhost/insert.php

Output:

Connect successfully! Select db successfully!

Insert data successfully!

Check database in PhpMyAdmin:

id	color1	color2	color3	color4
1	red	yellow	green	blue
2	pink	navy	purple	orange

Explanation:

"insert into colortable (color1, color2, color3, color4) value
(\"pink\",\"navy\",\"purple\",\"orange\");" inserts four strings into
four columns respectively.

"mysqli_query($con,$sql);" executes the query.

Note: In the PHP code, if we use MySQL command to insert
strings into a table, the strings should be enclosed by \" symbols.

For example: (\"pink\",\"navy\",\"purple\",\"orange\").

But if we want to insert numbers to the table, the numbers should
not be enclosed by \" symbols.

For example:

insert into mytable (n1, n2, n3, n4) value(1, 2, 3, 4);   Correct!

Alter Table Structure

The syntax to change the table structure is:

$sql="**alter** table tableName **add column** data type";

$query=**mysqli_query**($con, $sql);

$sql="alter table tableName add column data type" is used to add a new column to the table.

$query=mysqli_query($con, $sql) executes the query.

"$con" is the connection to MySql server. (See previous page).

Example 8.6

```php
<?php

require("select.php");    // import "select.php"

$sql="alter table colortable add column color5 varchar(20)";

$query=mysqli_query( $con, $sql);    // run query

if( $query ) {

echo  " Add columns successfully! ";

}

?>
```

Save this file with name "**alter.php**" to the working folder.

Please run this program by http://localhost/alter.php

Output:

Connect successfully! Select db successfully!
Add columns successfully!

Check database in PhpMyAdmin:

id	color1	color2	color3	color4	color5
1	red	yellow	green	blue	NULL
2	pink	navy	purple	orange	NULL

Explanation:

We can see the "color5" column in the table.

"alter table colortable add column color5 varchar(20)" adds a new column "color5" to table "colortable".

"mysqli_query($sql, $con);" performs the query.

Update Table Data (1)

The syntax to update a table is:

$sql="**update** tableName **set** columnName **where** id = int";

$query=**mysqli_query**($con, $sql);

"**update** tableName **set** columnName **where** id = int" can update the data value in a table.

$query=mysqli_query($con, $sql) executes the query.

"$con" is the connection to MySql server. (See previous page).

Example 8.7

```php
<?php

require("select.php");    // import "select.php"

$sql="update colortable set color5='sky' where id =1 ";

// set a value "sky" in the "color5" column

$query=mysqli_query( $con, $sql);    // run query

if( $query ) {

echo  " Update successfully! ";

}

?>
```

Save this file with name **"update1.php"** to the working folder.

Please run this program by http://localhost/update1.php

Output:

Connect successfully! Select db successfully!

Update successfully!

Check database in PhpMyAdmin:

id	color1	color2	color3	color4	color5
1	red	yellow	green	blue	sky
2	pink	navy	purple	orange	

Explanation:

We can see the "sky" in the "color5" column.

"update colortable set color5='sky' where id =1 " sets a value "sky" in the "color5" column where the id is 1 in "colortable".

Update Table Data (2)

In MySQL data table:

The row in the table is also known as "record".

The column in the table is also known as "field".

We can add data in the specified record or the specified field.

Example 8.8

```php
<?php

require("select.php");    // import "select.php"

$sql="update colortable set color5='olive' where id =2 ";

// set a value in the second record where id is 2

$query=mysqli_query( $con, $sql);    // run query

if( $query ) {

echo  " Update successfully! ";

}

?>
```

Save this file with name "update2.php" to the working folder.

Please run this program by http://localhost/update2.php

Output:

Connect successfully! Select db successfully!

Update successfully!

Check database in PhpMyAdmin:

id	color1	color2	color3	color4	color5
1	red	yellow	green	blue	sky
2	pink	navy	purple	orange	olive

Explanation:

We can see the "olive" in the "color5" column.

"update tableName **set** columnName **where** id = int" can update the data value in a table.

"update colortable set color5='olive' where id =2 " renews the color5 data to "olive" where the id is 2 in "colortable".

Retrieve Table Data

The syntax to retrieve table data is:

```
$sql="select column from tableName";

$query=mysqli_query($con, $sql);
```

$sql="select column from tableName" is used to retrieve table data by the column name from a table.

$query=mysqli_query($con, $sql) executes the query.

"$con" is the connection to MySql server. (See previous page).

mysqli_fetch_array( ) returns an array that contains rows of a table. (We will study this command later in detail.)

Example 8.9

Given colortable

id	color1	color2	color3	color4	color5
1	red	yellow	green	blue	sky
2	pink	navy	purple	orange	olive

```php
<?php

require("select.php");     // import "select.php"

$sql="select id, color1 from colortable";

$query=mysqli_query( $con,$sql );   // run query

if( $query ) {

echo  " Retrieve data successfully! <br>";

}

while($row = mysqli_fetch_array($query)){
```

```
// mysqli_fetch_array( ) returns an array that contains rows

echo("<br> ID: ".$row["id"]);

  // $row["id"] gets id numbers in each row

echo("<br> color1: ".$row["color1"]);

}    // $row["color1"] gets color1 values in each row

?>
```

Save this file with name **"retrieve.php"** to the working folder.

Please run this program by http://localhost/retrieve.php

Output:

Connect successfully! Select db successfully!
Retrieve data successfully!
ID: 1
color1: red
ID: 2
color1: pink

Explanation:

"select id, color1 from colortable" retrieves table data by the id and color1 from the colortable.

mysqli_query($con, $sql) performs the query.

mysqli_fetch_array( ) returns an array that contains rows of a table. (We will study this command later in detail.)

mysqli_fetch_row( )

The syntax of mysqli_fetch_row() is:

```
mysqli_fetch_row( );
```

"mysqli_fetch_row( )" returns an indexed array that contains the keys and values about columns and values in each row.

The element key the indexed array is always a number type.

e.g. [number] => value.

Example 8.10   Given colortable

id	color1	color2	color3	color4	color5
1	red	yellow	green	blue	sky
2	pink	navy	purple	orange	olive

```php
<?php
require("select.php");    // import "select.php"
$sql="select * from colortable";  // "*" represents all columns
$query=mysqli_query( $con, $sql);
while ( $array=mysqli_fetch_row ($query) ){
print_r($array);   // print_r( ) is used to print the array
echo "<br>";
}
?>
```

Save this file with name **"fetchrow.php"** to the working folder.

Please run this program by http://localhost/fetchrow.php

Connect successfully! Select db successfully!

Array ([0] => 1 [1] => red [2] => yellow [3] => green [4] => blue
[5] => sky)

Array ([0] => 2 [1] => pink [2] => navy [3] => purple [4] =>
orange [5] => olive)

Explanation:

"mysqli_fetch_row( )" returns an indexed array that contains the
keys and values about columns and values in each row.

One array represents one record in the table.

The element key the indexed array is always a number type.

print_r( ) is used to print array.

mysqli_fetch_assoc( )

The syntax of mysqli_fetch_assoc() is:

```
mysqli_fetch_assoc( );
```

"mysqli_fetch_assoc( )" returns an associative array that contains the keys and values about columns and values in each row.

The element key of associative array is always a string type.

e.g. [string]=> value.

Example 8.11   Given colortable

id	color1	color2	color3	color4	color5
1	red	yellow	green	blue	sky
2	pink	navy	purple	orange	olive

```php
<?php

require("select.php");     // import "select.php"

$sql="select * from colortable";  // "*" represents all columns

$query=mysqli_query( $con, $sql);

while ( $array=mysqli_fetch_assoc ($query) ){

print_r($array);   // print_r( ) is used to print the array

echo "<br>";

}
?>
```

Save this file with name **"fetchassoc.php"** to the working folder.

Please run this program by http://localhost/fetchassoc.php

Output:

Connect successfully! Select db successfully!

Array ([id] => 1 [color1] => red [color2] => yellow [color3] =>
green [color4] => blue [color5] => sky)

Array ([id] => 2 [color1] => pink [color2] => navy [color3] =>
purple [color4] => orange [color5] => olive)

Explanation:

"mysqli_fetch_assoc( )" returns an associative array that contains
the keys and values about columns and values in each row.

One array represents one record in the table.

The element key of associative array is always a string type.

print_r( ) is used to print the array.

mysqli_fetch_array( )

The syntax of mysqli_fetch_array() is:

```
mysqli_fetch_array( );
```

"mysqli_fetch_array( )" returns a indexed and associative array that contains the keys and values about columns and values in each row.

The element keys of array are both number type and string type.

e.g. [number]=>value   [string]=>value.

Example 8.12

Given colortable

id	color1	color2	color3	color4	color5
1	red	yellow	green	blue	sky
2	pink	navy	purple	orange	olive

```php
<?php

require("select.php");    // import "select.php"

$sql="select * from colortable";  // * represents all columns

$query=mysqli_query( $con, $sql);

$array=mysqli_fetch_array ($query);

print_r($array);    // print_r( ) is used to print array

?>
```

Save this file with name **"fetcharray.php"** to the working folder.

Please run this program by http://localhost/fetcharray.php

Output:

Array (

[0] => 1   [id] => 1

[1] => red   [color1] => red

[2] => yellow   [color2] => yellow

[3] => green   [color3] => green

[4] => blue   [color4] => blue

[5] => sky   [color5] => sky

)

Explanation:

"mysqli_fetch_array( )" returns a indexed and associative array that contains the keys and values about columns and values in each row.

The element keys of array are both number type and string type.

One array represents one record in the table.

print_r( ) is used to print the array.

mysqli_num_rows( )

The syntax of mysqli_num_rows() is:

```
mysqli_num_rows( $query );
```

mysqli_num_rows($query) returns the total number of rows of a table.

Example 8.13   Given colortable

id	color1	color2	color3	color4	color5
1	red	yellow	green	blue	sky
2	pink	navy	purple	orange	olive

```php
<?php
require("select.php");    // import "select.php"
$sql = "select * from colortable";  // "*" represents all columns
$query = mysqli_query($con, $sql);
$num = mysqli_num_rows( $query );
echo  ("The total number of rows is: $num");
?>
```

Save this file with name **"numrow.php"** to the working folder.

Please run this program by http://localhost/numrow.php

Outputs:

Connect successfully! Select db successfully!
The total number of rows is: 2

Explanation:

"$num=mysqli_num_rows($query)" returns the total number of rows of a table.

Because there are two rows in colortable, the output is 2.

mysqli_close( )

The syntax of mysqli_close() is:

```
mysqli_close( );
```

Closes an opened database connection.

Example 8.14

```php
<?php
$con= mysqli_connect( "localhost", "root", "12345678" );
mysqli_close($con);
echo "The connection is closed successfully!";
?>
```

Save this file with name "**close.php**" to the working folder.

Please run this program by http://localhost/close.php

Output:

The connection is closed successfully!

Explanation:

"**mysqli_close($con)**" closes an opened database connection.

mysqli_xxx_xxx ( ) Summary

Commands	Description
mysqli_affected_row ( )	Returns the number of row affected by query
mysqli_close ( )	Closes the connection with MySQL server
mysqli_connect ( )	Creates an initial connection with MySQL server
mysqli_create_db ( )	Creates a database on the MySQL server
mysqli_data_seek ( )	Adjusts the result pointer to a random row in the results
mysqli_db_query ( )	This function was deprecated in PHP 5.3.0
mysqli_error ( )	Returns a string with the error description
mysqli_fetch_array ( )	Returns an array related to the fetched row
mysqli_fetch_assoc ( )	Returns an associative array of fetched row
mysqli_fetch_row ( )	Returns an indexed array of the fetched row
mysqli_free_result ( )	Clears the system memory associated with the result
mysqli_get_server_info ( )	Returns a string with the MySQL server version
mysqli_num_rows ( )	Returns the number of rows in the result set
mysqli_query( )	Submits a query to the database on the server
mysqli_real_escape_string ( )	Escapes special characters in a string for MySQL
mysqli_result ( )	Returns a string of one cell from a MySQL result set
mysqli_select_db ( )	Selects the database to use by database name

Hands-on Project: Work Together

PHP with MySQL

Open an editor, input following codes to it:

```php
<?php

$con = mysqli_connect ( "localhost", "root", "12345678" );

if ($con) {   // connect MySQL server

echo " Connect successfully! ";

}

$select = mysqli_select_db ( $con, "mydb" );

if ($select) {   // "mydb" has been created in Chapter 7

echo " Select db successfully! <br><br>";

}

?>

<?php

$sql="select id, book1, book2, book3 from mytable";  // retrieve

$query=mysqli_query( $con,$sql );  // run query

if( $query ) {

echo  " Retrieve data successfully! <br>";

}

while($row = mysqli_fetch_array($query)){

// mysqli_fetch_array($query) returns an array named $row
```

173

```
echo("<br><br> ID: ".$row["id"]);

echo("<br> book1: ".$row["book1"]);

echo("<br> book2: ".$row["book2"]);

echo("<br> book3: ".$row["book3"]);

}

?>
```

Save this file with name **"phpmysql.php"** to the working folder.

Please run this program by http://localhost/phpmysql.php

Output:

Connect successfully! Select db successfully!

Retrieve data successfully!

ID: 1

book1: PHP

book2: JSP

book3: ASP

ID: 2

book1: LAMP

book2: J2EE

book3: HTML

Explanation:

"mysqli_connect ("localhost", "root", "12345678")" connects a MySQL server by using hostname, username and password.

"mysqli_select_db ($con, "mydb")" selects a database "mydb" by specifying a server and database name.

"mydb" has been created in Chapter 7 previously.

id	book1	book2	book3
1	PHP	JSP	ASP
2	LAMP	J2EE	HTML

"select id, book1, book2, book3 from mytable" retrieves table data by the id, book1, book2, and color3 from mytable.

"mysqli_query($con,$sql)" executes the query.

"mysqli_fetch_array( )" returns an array that contains the keys and values about columns and values in each row.

The values of $row["id"] are 1 or 2.

The values of $row[book1] are PHP or LAMP

The values of $row[book2] are JSP or J2EE

The values of $row[book3] are ASP or HTML

PHP MySQL

Q & A

Questions

Please choose the correct answer.

(1)

```php
<?php
fill in here multiply($x, $y){    // defines a function
calculate($x, $y);
}
fill in here calculate($a, $b){    // defines a function
$result = $a * $b;
echo("The value is $result");
}
?>
<?php
multiply(10,20);
?>
```

A. void   B. int   C. def   D. function

(2)

```php
<?php
echo "while statement: <br>";

$value1=1;

fill in here ($value1<=10){    // loop statement

echo $value1." ";

$value1++;

}

echo "<br><br>";

echo "do...while statement: <br>";

$value2=1;

fill in here {    // loop statement

echo $value2." ";

$value2++;

}while($value2<=10);

echo "<br><br>";

echo "for statement: <br>";

fill in here ($i=1;$i<=10;$i++){    // loop statement

$value3=$i;

echo $value3." ";

}
```

?>

A. while   do   for

B. switch   for   while

C. while   switch   for

D. for   do   while

(3)

```
<html>

<body>

<?

$a = array("zero", "one", "two");

echo "In array('zero', 'one', 'two'): <br><br>";

fill in here ($a as $key => $v){   // iterates through the array

echo "The number ".$key." element:  <br>";

echo "key is: ".$key.",   ";

echo "value is: ".$v. "<br><br><br>";

}

?>

</body>

</html>
```

A. while   B. do   C. foreach   D. for

(4)

```html
<html>

<p>Please Select Your Favorite Color</p>

<form method=get >

<input type="radio" name="color"

value="Red" >Red<br>

<input type="radio" name="color"

value="Yellow" >Yellow<br>

<input type="radio" name="color"

value="Green" >Green<br>

<br><br>

<input type="submit" value="Submit">

<br><br>

</form>

</html>

<?php

echo "You Select:<br><br>";
```

```php
$hobby = fill in here ['color'];    // gets the submitted data

echo($hobby);

?>
```

A. $_POST

B. $_GET

C. $_FILES

D. $_ENV

(5)

```php
<?php

fill in here ( "Location: http://www.amazon.com") ;

// redirects to www.amazon.com.

?>
```

A. url   B. redirect   C. function   D. header

(6)

```php
<?php
class Flower{        // class definition
var $c = "Flower is beautiful";
function beautify() {
echo $this->c;      // $this represents $obj
}
}
$obj= fill in here Flower();     // creates an object
$obj->beautify();
?>
```

A. Object   B. create   C. new   D. Class

(7)

MySQL Commands	Description
SELECT field fill in here table WHERE condition	query data
INSERT fill in here table (field) VALUES (value)	insert data
UPDATE table fill in here field = value WHERE condition	update data

A. INTO   FROM   SET

B. FROM   INTO   SET

C. INTO   SET   FROM

D. SET   FROM   INTO

(8)

```php
<?php
$con= fill in here ( "localhost", "root", "12345678" );
// connects MySQL server
if( $con ) {
echo " Connect successfully! ";
}
?>
```

A. mysqli_connect

B. mysqli

C. connect

D. server

(9)

```php
 <?php

$select = fill in here ( $con, "study" );

// selects a database "study".

if( $select ) {

echo  " Select db successfully! ";

}

?>
```

A. mysqli

B. select

C. db.

D. mysqli_select_db

(10)

```php
<?php

$sql=" fill in here into colortable (color1, color2, color3, color4)
value (\"pink\",\"navy\",\"purple\",\"orange\")";

// inserts table data

$query=mysqli_query( $con,$sql);
```

```php
if( $query ) {

echo " Insert data successfully! ";

}

?>
```

A. add   B. put   C. insert   D. include

(11)

```php
<?php
function test ($a, $b, $c){

$sum=$a+$b+$c;

echo $sum;

}

fill in here (3, 6, 9);    // call the function test()

?>
```

A. call   B. test   C. function   D. return

(12)

```php
<?php
$number=20;
fill in here ( $number ) {   // compare $number with case value
case 10 : echo "Running case 10";  break;
case 20 : echo "Running case 20";  break;
case 30 : echo "Running case 30";  break;
default :  echo "Running default code";  break;  }
?>
```

A. switch   B. for   C. while   D. do

(13)

```php
<?php
$color =array("yellow", "red", "blue", "white");
fill in here ( $color );    // sort array elements
foreach( $color as $value ) { echo "$value ";}
?>
```

A. array_sort   B. arrange   C. $sort   D. sort

(14)

```
<form fill in here ="myfile.php" method="get">
// specifies "myfile.php" to process data
<input type="text" name="information">
</form>
```

A. name   B. action   C. act   D. id

(15)

```
<?php
$filename = "myfile.txt";
$openfile = fopen( $filename, w );
$content = fill in here ( $openfile, "Hello World!" );
// writes "Hello World!" to specified file.
?>
```

A. write   B. input   C. fwrite   D. enter

(16)

class animal{

// parent class definition

}

class dog **fill in here** animal{   // define a child class "dog"

// sub class definition

}

class cat **fill in here** animal{   // define a child class "cat"

// sub class definition.

}

A. extends

B. inheritance

C. inherit

D. extend

(17)

MySQL Commands	Descriptions
<u>fill in</u> DATABASE databaseName	create a database
<u>fill in</u> databaseName	use a database
<u>fill in</u> databaseName	show a database
<u>fill in</u> databaseName	remove a database

    A. DROP   SHOW   USE   CREATE

    B. USE   CREATE   SHOW   DROP

    C. CREATE   USE   DROP   SHOW

    D. CREATE   USE   SHOW   DROP

(18)

```php
<?php

$sql=" fill in table colortable add column color5 varchar(20)";

// adds a new column "color5" to table "colortable"

$query=mysqli_query( $con, $sql);

if( $query ) {
```

189

```php
echo  " Add columns successfully! ";

}

?>
```

A. add   B. alter   C. modify   D. change

(19)

```
use study;     # use database "study"

fill in color2 from colortable;

 # shows data of color2 only from colortable.
```

A. show   B. alter   C. select   D. update

(20)

```php
<?php

$con= mysqli_connect( "localhost", "root", "12345678" );

// ....some PHP code...
```

__fill in here__ **($con)**;   // close an opened database connection to MySql server.

?>

A. close   B. end   C. exit   D. mysqli_close

(21)

```php
<?php
function test( fill in here ){    /* declare a function with arguments   */
echo ("$arg");
}
test("display a sample");  // call the function, pass args.
?>
```

A. $argument

B. $arg

C. &argument

D. &arg

(22)

```php
<?php
function multiply($x, $y){
fill in here $x * $y;   // pass the result value to function caller
}
?>
<?php
$result = multiply(10,20);   // this is a function caller
echo $result;
?>
```

A. pass   B. send   C. return   D. continue

(23)

```php
<?php
$array1=array ("A", "B", "C");
$array2=array ("D", "E", "F");
$array = fill in here ( $array1, $array2 );   // merge arrays
```

```
foreach( $array as $value) { echo("$value " );}

?>
```

A. merge

B. array.merge

C. array_merge

D. combine

(24)

```
<html>

<body>

<form action="postDemo.php " method="post">

<input type="text" name="information"> <!--user input -->

</form>

<?php

$myData = fill in here [ information ]; // get input from user

echo ("You have inputted: ".$myData);      // show input

?>

</body>

</html>
```

A. $_POST

B. $_GET

C. $_FILES

D. $_ENV

(25)

// firstPage.php

```php
<?php fill in here()?>    // start php session
```

Here is "First Page".

Send Out a Session ID


```
<a href = "secondPage.php?<?php echo(SID);?>">To Second
Page </a>
 <!- - pass session id to secondPage.php- ->
```

A. session

B. start

C. session.start

D. session_start

(26)

```php
<?php
class Flower{
var $c;
function fill in here( $arg ) {     // define a constructor
$this->c= $arg;   //constructor is used to initialize variable.
echo $this->c;
}}
$obj= new Flower( yellow );
?>
```

A. construct

B. __construct

C. constructor

D. __constructor

(27)

MySQL Commands	Descriptions
<u>fill in here</u> TABLE tableName	create a table
<u>fill in here</u> TABLE	show all tables
<u>fill in here</u> TABLE tableName	change data of a field
<u>fill in here</u> TABLE tableName	remove a table

A. CREATE   SHOW   CHANGE   REMOVE

B. NEW   DISPLAY   ALTER   DELETE

C. NEW   DISPLAY   ALTER   REMOVE

D. CREATE   SHOW   ALTER   DROP

(28)

```php
<?php
$sql="select * from colortable";
$query=mysqli_query( $con, $sql);
$array=mysqli_fetch_ fill in here($query);
// return an array, its element key is always number type
print_r($array);
?>
```

A. index   B. array   C. row   D. assoc

(29)

```php
<?php
$filename = "myfile.txt";
$openfile = fopen( $filename, r );
$content = fill in here ( $openfile, 20 );   /* read 20 bytes from myfile.txt */
echo "$content";
?>
```

A. read

B. fread

C. readFile

D. fileRead

(30)

```php
<?php
class A{
function display( ) {
echo "A function is called <br>";
}}
class B extends A{
function show(){
A fill in here display( );    // class A calls a function
echo "B function is called <br>";
}}
B fill in here show( );    // class B calls a function
?>
```

A. ::   B. ->   C. :   D. .

(31)

SQL Modifier	Descriptions
fill in here	can be empty value
fill in here	cannot not duplicate any entry
fill in here	specify a default value for a field

fill in here	specify an index field for table

A. EMPTY   EXCLUSIVE   DEFAULT   KEY

B. BLANK   UNIQUE   VALUE   INDEX

C. NULL   SOLE   DEFAULT   KEY

D. NULL   UNIQUE   DEFAULT   INDEX

(32)

```php
<?php

$sql="select * from colortable";   // * represents all columns

$query=mysqli_query( $con, $sql);

$array=mysqli_fetch_ fill in here ($query);

// return an array, its element key is always string type

print_r($array);   // print_r( ) is used to print array

?>
```

A. index   B. array   C. row   D. assoc

Answers

01	D	17	D
02	A	18	B
03	C	19	C
04	B	20	D
05	D	21	B
06	C	22	C
07	B	23	C
08	A	24	A
09	D	25	D
10	C	26	B
11	B	27	D
12	A	28	C
13	D	29	B
14	B	30	A
15	C	31	D
16	A	32	D

Recommended Books by Ray Yao

(**Note:** Each Cheat Sheet contains more than 300 examples, more than 300 outputs, and more than 300 explanations.)

Part Two

Real World Code

& Explanations

Paperback Books by Ray Yao

C# Cheat Sheet

C++ Cheat Sheet

JAVA Cheat Sheet

JavaScript Cheat Sheet

PHP MySQL Cheat Sheet

Python Cheat Sheet

Html Css Cheat Sheet

MySQL Cheat Sheet

SQL Cheat Sheet

Linux Command Line

Kindle Books by Ray Yao

C# Cheat Sheet

C++ Cheat Sheet

JAVA Cheat Sheet

JavaScript Cheat Sheet

PHP MySQL Cheat Sheet

Python Cheat Sheet

Html Css Cheat Sheet

MySQL Cheat Sheet

SQL Cheat Sheet

Linux Command Line

(**Note:** Each Cheat Sheet contains more than 300 examples, more than 300 outputs, and more than 300 explanations.)

01. The Greenwich Mean Time

```php
<?php
$hr = gmdate( "H" );
$gmt = gmdate( "H:i a" );
if( $hr >= 00 && $hr < 12 ) { $msg = "It is morning there. "; }
if( $hr >= 12 && $hr < 18 ) { $msg = "It is afternoon there. "; }
if( $hr >= 18 && $hr < 24 ) { $msg = "It is evening there. ";}
echo( "The Greenwich Mean Time is $gmt <br>" );
echo( " $msg " );
?>
```

Output:

The Greenwich Mean Time is 06:18 am

It is morning there.

Explanation:

$hr = gmdate("H");

This code uses the gmdate function to get the current hour (in 24-hour format) in Greenwich Mean Time (GMT) and assigns it to the variable $hr.

$gmt = gmdate("H:i a");

This code uses gmdate again to get the current time in GMT in the format "hour:minute AM/PM" and assigns it to the variable $gmt.

The code then uses a series of if statements to determine the time of day based on the value of $hr (the current hour in GMT).

if ($hr >= 00 && $hr < 12) { $msg = "It is morning there. "; }

If the current hour is greater than or equal to 00 and less than 12, it sets the variable $msg to "It is morning there."

if ($hr >= 12 && $hr < 18) { $msg = "It is afternoon there. "; }

If the current hour is greater than or equal to 12 and less than 18, it sets the variable $msg to "It is afternoon there."

if ($hr >= 18 && $hr < 24) { $msg = "It is evening there. "; }

If the current hour is greater than or equal to 18 and less than 24, it sets the variable $msg to "It is evening there."

**echo("The Greenwich Mean Time is $gmt
");**

This code prints the current GMT time in the format "hour:minute AM/PM" using the value stored in the $gmt variable.

echo(" $msg ");

This code prints the message stored in the $msg variable, which was determined based on the current hour in GMT.

02. Create some random numbers

```php
<?php
  srand(time());

  $num1 = rand( 1, 36 );

  $num2 = rand( 1, 36 );

  $num3 = rand( 1, 36 );

  $num4 = rand( 1, 36 );

  $num5 = rand( 1, 36 );

  $num6 = rand( 1, 36 );

  echo( "The lottery numbers are:<br>" );

  echo ($num1." ".$num2." ".$num3." ".$num4." ".$num5."
".$num6 );

 ?>
```

Output:

The lottery numbers are:

10 2 35 23 6 18

Explanation:

srand(time());

This code seeds the random number generator with the current
timestamp (the result of the time() function). Seeding the random

number generator with a changing value (like the current time) helps ensure that the random numbers generated are different each time the script is run.

$num1 = rand(1, 36);

This code generates a random integer between 1 and 36 (inclusive) and assigns it to the variable $num1. This represents the first lottery number.

Similar to the previous line, there are five more lines of code ($num2, $num3, $num4, $num5, and $num6) that generate random numbers for the remaining lottery numbers.

**echo("The lottery numbers are:
");**

This code prints a message indicating that the following numbers are lottery numbers. The <br> tag is used to insert a line break, so the numbers will appear on separate lines in the output.

echo($num1." ".$num2." ".$num3." ".$num4." ".$num5." ".$num6);

This code prints the six random numbers generated earlier, separated by spaces. The . operator is used for concatenation, combining the numbers and spaces into a single string to be displayed.

03, Arithmetical calculation

Source Code 03

```php
<?php

$x = 100; $y = 2;

$sum = $x + $y;

$dif = $x - $y;

$pro = $x * $y;

$quo = $x / $y;

echo ("$x + $y =  $sum<br>");

echo ("$x - $y =  $dif<br>");

echo ("$x * $y =  $pro<br>");

echo ("$x / $y =  $quo<br>");

?>
```

Output:

```
100 + 2 = 102

100 - 2 = 98

100 * 2 = 200

100 / 2 = 50
```

Explanation:

This PHP code performs basic arithmetic operations on two variables, $x and $y, and then displays the results. Let's break down each part of the code:

$x = 100; $y = 2;

These lines initialize two variables, $x and $y. $x is set to 100, and $y is set to 2.

$sum = $x + $y;

This code calculates the sum of $x and $y and assigns the result to the variable $sum. In this case, it's performing the addition operation, so $sum will hold the value 100 + 2, which is 102.

$dif = $x - $y;

This code calculates the difference between $x and $y and assigns the result to the variable $dif. It performs the subtraction operation, so $dif will hold the value 100 - 2, which is 98.

$pro = $x * $y;

This code calculates the product of $x and $y and assigns the result to the variable $pro. It performs the multiplication operation, so $pro will hold the value 100 * 2, which is 200.

$quo = $x / $y;

This code calculates the quotient of dividing $x by $y and assigns the result to the variable $quo. It performs the division operation, so $quo will hold the value 100 / 2, which is 50.

The code then uses echo statements to display the results of these calculations:

**echo ("$x + $y = $sum
");**

This code prints the addition result in the format "100 + 2 = 102" with a line break (<br>) for formatting.

**echo ("$x - $y = $dif
");**

This code prints the subtraction result in the format "100 - 2 = 98" with a line break.

**echo ("$x * $y = $pro
");**

This code prints the multiplication result in the format "100 * 2 = 200" with a line break.

**echo ("$x / $y = $quo
");**

This code prints the division result in the format "100 / 2 = 50" with a line break.

04. Reverse a number

Source Code 04

```php
<?php

$number = 987654321;

$reverse = 0;

$num = $number;

while(floor($number)){

$mod = $number%10;

$reverse = $reverse * 10 + $mod;

$number = $number/10;

}

echo "The reverse of $num is: $reverse.";

?>
```

The reverse of 987654321 is: 123456789.

This PHP code is designed to reverse a given number. Let's break down each part of the code:

$number = 987654321;

This code initializes the variable $number with the value 987654321. This is the number that will be reversed.

$reverse = 0;

This code initializes the variable $reverse to 0. This variable will be used to store the reversed number.

$num = $number;

This code creates a copy of the original number and assigns it to the variable $num. This copy will be used later to display the original number in the output.

The code has a while loop with the condition

while(floor($number))

This loop will continue as long as the integer part (floor) of $number is not zero. In other words, the loop will keep running until all digits of the original number have been processed.

Inside the loop:

$mod = $number % 10

This code calculates the remainder of dividing $number by 10, which gives us the last digit of the number.

$reverse = $reverse * 10 + $mod;

This code appends the last digit ($mod) to the reverse variable, effectively building the reversed number. It multiplies the current reversed number by 10 and then adds the last digit.

$number = $number / 10;

This code divides $number by 10 to remove the last digit. This prepares the next iteration of the loop to process the next digit.

Once the while loop completes, it means that all the digits of the original number have been reversed, and the reversed number is stored in the $reverse variable.

echo "The reverse of $num is: $reverse.";

This code prints the original number ($num) and its reversed counterpart ($reverse) in a human-readable format.

05. Reverse a string

```php
<?php

$str = "Mirror picture";

echo "$str  :  " .strrev ( $str );

?>
```

Output:

Mirror picture : erutcip rorriM

Explanation:

This PHP code reverses a given string. Let's break down each part of the code:

$str = "Mirror picture";

This code initializes the variable $str with the string "Mirror picture." This is the string that will be reversed.

215

echo "$str : " . strrev($str);

This code prints the original string followed by its reverse. Here's what each part of this code does:

echo

This is a PHP function used to output text.

"$str: "

This part of the echo statement is a string that includes the original string ($str) followed by two colons and spaces. This is just for formatting the output and making it more human-readable. The result will look like: "Mirror picture : ".

.strrev($str)

This part of the echo statement uses the strrev() function to reverse the string stored in the variable $str. The strrev() function takes a string as input and returns the reverse of that string.

"."

The dot operator (.) is used for concatenation, which combines the first string with the reversed string.

06. Swap two numbers

Source Code 06

```php
<?php

echo "Before exchanging:<br>";

$x = 10;  $y = 20;

echo "x = $x<br>";

echo "y = $y<br>";

echo "After exchanging:<br>";

$temp = $x;

$x = $y;  $y = $temp;

echo "x = $x<br>";

echo "y = $y<br>";

?>
```

Output:

Before exchanging:

x = 10

y = 20

After exchanging:

x = 20

y = 10

Explanation:

This PHP code demonstrates how to exchange the values of two variables $x and $y using a temporary variable. Let's break down each part of the code:

**echo "Before exchanging:
";**

This code is an echo statement that prints the text "Before exchanging:" followed by a line break (<br>). This is used for formatting purposes to indicate that the values of $x and $y will be displayed before they are swapped.

$x = 10; $y = 20;

These lines initialize two variables, $x and $y, with the values 10 and 20, respectively.

**echo "x = $x
";**

This code prints the value of $x along with a line break to display it in the output.

**echo "y = $y
";**

This code prints the value of $y along with a line break to display it in the output.

**echo "After exchanging:
";**

This code is another echo statement that indicates, with a line break, that the values of $x and $y are about to be exchanged.

$temp = $x;

This code creates a temporary variable $temp and assigns it the value of $x. This step is essential to store one of the values temporarily before swapping them.

$x = $y; $y = $temp;

These lines perform the actual value exchange.

$x is assigned the value of $y, which means it now holds the value 20.

$y is assigned the value of $temp, which was the original value of $x (i.e., 10).

Finally, the code prints the values of $x and $y after the exchange using echo statements:

**echo "x = $x
";**

Prints the new value of $x (which is 20) with a line break.

**echo "y = $y
";**

This code prints the new value of $y (which is 10) with a line break.

As we can see, the values of $x and $y have been successfully exchanged using a temporary variable.

07. Check prime number

Source Code 07

```php
<?php
$number = 5;
$limit=0;
for ( $n=1; $n<=$number; $n++) {
if (($number%$n)==0) {
$limit++;
}
}
if ($limit<3) {
echo "$number is a prime number.";
}
else{
echo "$number is not a prime number.";
}
?>
```

5 is a prime number.

Explanation:

This PHP code is used to determine whether a given number is prime or not.

Let's go through each part of the code step by step:

$number = 5;

$limit=0;

Declaration and assignment of two variables, $number and $limit. $number is assigned the value 5, $limit is assigned the value 0.

for ($n=1; $n<=$number; $n++) {

Start of a for loop. It initializes a variable $n to 1, runs the loop as long as $n is less than or equal to $number (which is 5 in this case), and increments $n in each iteration.

if (($number%$n)==0) {

Inside the loop, this line checks if the remainder of dividing $number by $n is equal to 0. If true, it means that $n is a factor of $number.

$limit++;

If the condition in the previous if statement is true, increment the $limit variable by 1. This is used to count the number of factors.

if ($limit<3) {

This line checks if the value of $limit is less than 3. If true, it means that the number has fewer than three factors, indicating that it's a prime number.

echo "$number is a prime number.";

If the condition in the previous if statement is true, this line prints the message indicating that $number is a prime number.

} else {

If the condition in the if statement is false, this line marks the beginning of the else block.

echo "$number is not a prime number.";

Inside the else block, this line prints the message indicating that $number is not a prime number.

In summary, the PHP program checks whether the variable $number (which is 5 in this case) is a prime number and prints the corresponding message based on the result of the primality test.

08. Check if a string contains a specified word

Source Code 08

```php
<?php

$myStr = 'This is a PHP programming book';

$word = "PHP";

if (strpos($myStr, $word) == true) {

echo "The string contains $word";

}

else {

echo "The string does not contain $word";

}

?>
```

The string contains PHP

This PHP code is used to check if a given string contains a specific word ("PHP" in this case). Here's an explanation of each part of the code:

$myStr = 'This is a PHP programming book';

This code initializes a variable called $myStr with a string containing the text "This is a PHP programming book." This is the string in which we want to check for the presence of the word "PHP."

$word = "PHP";

This code initializes another variable called $word with the word "PHP." This is the word that we want to check if it exists in the $myStr string.

if (strpos($myStr, $word) == true) {

This code uses the strpos function to check if the word $word exists in the string $myStr. Here's how it works:

strpos($myStr, $word)

The strpos function searches for the position of the first occurrence of $word within $myStr. If it finds a match, it returns the position (an integer) where the match starts. If it doesn't find a match, it returns false.

== true

This part checks if the result of strpos is equal to true. This is a type-strict comparison, meaning it checks if the result is both true and of the same data type (boolean).

If strpos finds a match (i.e., the word "PHP" is found in $myStr), the code inside the if block is executed:

echo "The string contains $word";

This code prints the message "The string contains PHP."

If strpos does not find a match (i.e., the word "PHP" is not found in $myStr), the code inside the else block is executed:

echo "The string does not contain $word";

This code prints the message "The string does not contain PHP."

This means that the word "PHP" is found within the $myStr string. If we were to change the value of $word to something that doesn't exist in $myStr, the output would be the message in the else block.

09. The area of a triangle

Source Code 09

```php
<?php

$h = 8;

$b = 12;

echo "The height of the triangle is $h<br>";

echo "The base of the triangle is $b<br>";

echo "The area of the triangle is " . ($b * $h) / 2;

?>
```

The height of the triangle is 8

The base of the triangle is 12

The area of the triangle is 48

This PHP code calculates and displays the area of a triangle given its height and base. Let's go through each part of the code step by step:

$h = 8;

This code initializes a variable $h with the value 8, which represents the height of the triangle.

$b = 12;

This code initializes another variable $b with the value 12, which represents the base of the triangle.

**echo "The height of the triangle is $h
";**

This code uses the echo statement to display the height of the triangle. The value of $h is inserted into the string using double quotes, and <br> is used for a line break.

**echo "The base of the triangle is $b
";**

Similarly, this code uses echo to display the base of the triangle, with the value of $b inserted into the string.

echo "The area of the triangle is " . ($b * $h) / 2;

This code calculates and displays the area of the triangle.

Here's how it works:

($b * $h)

This part calculates the product of the base $b and the height $h, which is the area of the triangle (since the area of a triangle is given by (base * height) / 2).

($b * $h) / 2

This part divides the product by 2 to get the final area value.

"The area of the triangle is " . ($b * $h) / 2;

This concatenates the area value with the string "The area of the triangle is " and then prints the result.

The output displays the height, base, and area of the triangle, with the area being calculated and shown as 48 based on the provided values of h and b.

10. The area of a rectangle

Source Code 10

```php
<?php

$l = 20;

$w = 30;

echo "The length of the rectangle is $l<br>";

echo "The width of the rectangle is $w<br>";

echo "The area of the rectangle is " . ($l * $w) ;

?>
```

The length of the rectangle is 20

The width of the rectangle is 30

The area of the rectangle is 600

Explanation:

This PHP code calculates and displays the area of a rectangle given its length and width. Let's go through each part of the code step by step:

$l = 20;

This code initializes a variable $l with the value 20, which represents the length of the rectangle.

$w = 30;

This code initializes another variable $w with the value 30, which represents the width of the rectangle.

**echo "The length of the rectangle is $l
";**

This code uses the echo statement to display the length of the rectangle. The value of $l is inserted into the string using double quotes.

**echo "The width of the rectangle is $w
";**

Similarly, this code uses echo to display the width of the rectangle, with the value of $w inserted into the string.

echo "The area of the rectangle is " . ($l * $w);

This code calculates and displays the area of the rectangle. Here's how it works:

($l * $w)

This part calculates the product of the length $l and the width $w, which is the area of the rectangle.

"The area of the rectangle is " . ($l * $w);

This concatenates the area value with the string "The area of the rectangle is " and then prints the result.

The output displays the length, width, and area of the rectangle, with the area being calculated and shown as 600 based on the provided values of l and w.

11. Print a triangle pattern

Source Code 11

```php
<?php

for($n=0;$n<=6;$n++){

for($m=1;$m<=$n;$m++){

echo "* ";

}

echo "<br>";

}

?>
```

Output:

```
*
*  *
*  *  *
*  *  *  *
*  *  *  *  *
*  *  *  *  *  *  *
```

Explanation:

The code is a PHP program that uses nested for loops to generate a pattern of asterisks (*).

Let's break down the code step by step:

for($n=0;$n<=6;$n++){

This is the outer for loop. It initializes a variable $n to 0 and runs the loop as long as $n is less than or equal to 6. The loop will execute 7 times (0 to 6).

for($m=1;$m<=$n;$m++){

This is the inner for loop. It initializes a variable $m to 1 and runs the loop as long as $m is less than or equal to the current value of $n. The number of times this loop executes depends on the value of $n in the outer loop.

233

echo "* ";

Inside the inner loop, this code prints an asterisk followed by a space.

echo "<br>";

After the inner loop completes, this code prints a line break (<br>), which causes the output to move to the next line.

So, let's see how this code works through the iterations:

When $n is 0, the inner loop doesn't execute because $m is already greater than $n. So, nothing is printed on the first line.

When $n is 1, the inner loop executes once, and an asterisk is printed on the second line.

When $n is 2, the inner loop executes twice, and two asterisks are printed on the third line.

This pattern continues until $n reaches 6, where the inner loop executes six times, and six asterisks are printed on the seventh line.

The final output of this code will be a pattern of asterisks, forming a right-angled triangle. Each line has a different number of asterisks based on the value of $n.

12. Print a diamond pattern

```php
<?php
echo "<pre>";
for ($x = 1; $x < 5; $x++) {
   for ($y = $x; $y < 5; $y++)
      echo "  ";
   for ($y = 2 * $x - 1; $y > 0; $y--)
      echo ("* ");
   echo "<br>";
}
$n = 5;
for ($x = 5; $x > 0; $x--) {
   for ($y = $n - $x; $y > 0; $y--)
      echo "  ";
   for ($y = 2 * $x - 1; $y > 0; $y--)
      echo ("* ");
   echo "<br>";
}
echo "</pre>";
?>
```

Output:

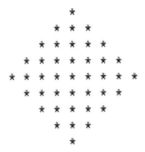

Explanation:

This PHP code generates a diamond pattern made of asterisks and spaces. It uses nested for loops to create the pattern. Let's break down the code step by step:

echo "<pre>";

This code sets the HTML rendering mode to "pre," which preserves whitespace formatting, allowing the pattern to display correctly.

for ($x = 1; $x < 5; $x++) {

This is the outer for loop, which starts with $x at 1 and runs as long as $x is less than 5. It controls the top half of the diamond.

```php
for ($y = $x; $y < 5; $y++)

echo "  ";
```

This loop adds spaces before the asterisks. The number of spaces depends on the value of $x. It starts with 2 spaces for the first line and decreases by 1 for each subsequent line.

```php
for ($y = 2 * $x - 1; $y > 0; $y--)

echo ("* ");
```

This loop prints asterisks followed by spaces. The number of asterisks depends on the value of $x. It starts with 1 asterisk for the first line and increases by 2 for each subsequent line.

```php
echo "<br>";
```

This code adds a line break to move to the next line after each row of the diamond.

After the top half of the diamond is created, the code continues with the following part:

```php
$n = 5;
```

This code sets $n to 5, which is used to control the number of spaces before the asterisks in the bottom half of the diamond.

```php
for ($x = 5; $x > 0; $x--) {
```

This is another outer for loop, but this time it counts down from 5 to 1. It controls the bottom half of the diamond.

```
for ($y = $n - $x; $y > 0; $y--)
```

```
echo "  ";
```

This loop adds spaces before the asterisks in the bottom half. The number of spaces decreases as $x decreases.

```
for ($y = 2 * $x - 1; $y > 0; $y--)
```

```
echo ("* ");
```

This loop prints asterisks followed by spaces in the bottom half. The number of asterisks increases as $x decreases.

```
echo "<br>";
```

This code adds a line break to move to the next line after each row in the bottom half.

```
echo "</pre>";
```

This code closes the "pre" tag, ending the whitespace-preserving formatting.

13. The sum from 1 to 100

Source Code 13

```php
<?php

for($n=0; $n<=100; $n++){

$sum = $sum + $n;

}

echo $sum;

?>
```

Output:

5050

Explanation:

This PHP code calculates the sum of all integers from 0 to 100 using a for loop and then prints the result. Let's break down the code step by step:

for ($n = 0; $n <= 100; $n++) {

This is a for loop that initializes a variable $n to 0. The loop continues as long as $n is less than or equal to 100. It iterates through all integers from 0 to 100.

$sum = $sum + $n;

Inside the loop, this code adds the current value of $n to the variable $sum. The variable $sum is used to accumulate the sum of all the numbers from 0 to 100.

The loop will execute 101 times (from 0 to 100), and in each iteration, it adds the current value of $n to the running total stored in $sum.

"}":

This closes the for loop.

echo $sum;

After the loop completes, this code prints the final value of $sum, which is the sum of all integers from 0 to 100.

When we run this code, it will calculate and print the sum of the numbers from 0 to 100, which is 5050.

14. Conversion between bin & dec

Source Code 14

```php
<?php
echo "Convert binary to decimal:<br>";
echo "1001=".bindec("1001") . "<br>";
echo "10101000=".bindec("10101000")."<br>";
echo "Convert decimal to binary:<br>";
echo "9=".decbin("9")."<br>";
echo "168=".decbin("168") . "<br>";
?>
```

Output:

Convert binary to decimal:

1001=9

10101000=168

Convert decimal to binary:

9=1001

168=10101000

This PHP code demonstrates how to convert binary numbers to decimal and decimal numbers to binary using the bindec() and decbin() functions.

Let's go through each part of the code:

echo "Convert binary to decimal:
";

This code prints a message indicating that we are converting binary to decimal.

echo "1001=".bindec("1001") . "<br>";

Here, we're converting the binary number "1001" to decimal using the bindec() function. It calculates the decimal equivalent of the binary number and then prints both the binary input and its decimal equivalent. In this case, "1001" in binary is equivalent to 9 in decimal, so it prints "1001=9" as the output.

echo "10101000=".bindec("10101000")."
";

Similarly, this code converts the binary number "10101000" to decimal. It calculates that "10101000" in binary is equivalent to 168 in decimal, so it prints "10101000=168" as the output.

echo "Convert decimal to binary:
";

This code prints a message indicating that we are converting decimal to binary.

**echo "9=".decbin("9")."
";**

Here, we're converting the decimal number 9 to binary using the decbin() function. It calculates the binary representation of the decimal number and then prints both the decimal input and its binary equivalent. In this case, 9 in decimal is equivalent to "1001" in binary, so it prints "9=1001" as the output.

echo "168=".decbin("168") . "<br>";

Similarly, this code converts the decimal number 168 to binary. It calculates that 168 in decimal is equivalent to "10101000" in binary, so it prints "168=10101000" as the output.

When we run this code, it will perform these binary-to-decimal and decimal-to-binary conversions and display the results as shown in the comments above each line.

15. Conversion between miles & kilometers

Source Code 15

```php
<?php
$ratio = 1.609344;
$m = 100;
$k = 100;
echo "100 miles = ".$m * $ratio." kilometers <br>";
echo "100 kilometers = ".$k / $ratio." miles <br>";
?>
```

Output:

100 miles = 160.9344 kilometers

100 kilometers = 62.137119223733 miles

Explanation:

This PHP code is a simple example of converting between miles and kilometers using a conversion ratio. Let's break down each part of the code:

$ratio = 1.609344;

This code sets a variable $ratio to the conversion factor from miles to kilometers. There are approximately 1.609344 kilometers in a mile.

$m = 100;

$k = 100;

These lines set two variables, $m and $k, to 100. This represents 100 miles and 100 kilometers, respectively, for the conversion examples.

**echo "100 miles = ".$m * $ratio." kilometers
";**

Here, it calculates the equivalent distance in kilometers for 100 miles by multiplying 100 (miles) by the conversion factor $ratio. It then prints the result in the form "100 miles = X kilometers," where X is the calculated value.

**echo "100 kilometers = ".$k / $ratio." miles
";**

Similarly, this code calculates the equivalent distance in miles for 100 kilometers by dividing 100 (kilometers) by the conversion factor $ratio. It then prints the result in the form "100 kilometers = Y miles," where Y is the calculated value.

When we run this code, it will perform these conversions using the specified conversion factor and display the results:

100 miles = 160.9344 kilometers

100 kilometers = 62.137119223733 miles

So, 100 miles is approximately equal to 160.9344 kilometers, and 100 kilometers is approximately equal to 62.1371 miles, based on the provided conversion ratio.

16. The largest number among three numbers

```php
<?php
    $n1=139;
    $n2=168;
    $n3=93;
    if($n1>$n2 && $n1>$n3) {
      echo "The largest number is: ".$n1;
    }
    else{
      if($n2>$n1 && $n2>$n3) {
        echo "The largest number is: ".$n2;
      }
      else
        echo "The largest number is: ".$n3;
    }
?>
```

The largest number is: 168

Explanation:

This PHP code determines and prints the largest number among three given variables: $n1, $n2, and $n3. It uses nested if-else statements to compare the values and identify the largest one. Let's break down the code step by step:

$n1 = 139;

$n2 = 168;

$n3 = 93;

These lines initialize three variables with numeric values.

if ($n1 > $n2 && $n1 > $n3) {

echo "The largest number is: " . $n1;

}

This is the first conditional statement. It checks if $n1 is greater than both $n2 and $n3. If it is, it prints a message indicating that $n1 is the largest number.

If the condition in the first if statement is not met, the code proceeds to the else block:

else {

if($n2>$n1 && $n2>$n3) {

Inside the else block, this line starts another if statement, checking if $n2 is greater than both $n1 and $n3.

echo "The largest number is: ".$n2;

If the condition in the inner if statement is true, this line prints the message indicating that $n2 is the largest number.

else

echo "The largest number is: ".$n3;

If the condition in the inner if statement is false, this line prints the message indicating that $n3 is the largest number. The closing braces indicate the end of the else block and the end of the PHP code.

In summary, this PHP program compares three numbers ($n1, $n2, and $n3) and prints a message indicating which one is the largest. It uses nested if statements to determine the largest number among the three.

17. Count characters & words

Source Code 17

```php
<?php
$str = "It is a pen";
echo "$str<br>";
$char = strlen($str) - substr_count($str, ' ');
echo ("Total ".$char." characters<br>");
$words = str_word_count($str);
echo ("Total ".$words." words<br>");
?>
```

Output:

It is a pen

Total 8 characters

Total 4 words

Explanation:

This PHP code operates on a given string, $str, and performs three operations to calculate and display information about the string.

Let's go through each part of the code:

$str = "It is a pen";

This code initializes the variable $str with the string "It is a pen."

**echo "$str
";**

Here, it simply prints the string stored in the variable $str, followed by a line break (<br>).

$char = strlen($str) - substr_count($str, ' ');

This code calculates the total number of characters in the string, excluding spaces. It does this in two steps:

strlen($str) calculates the length of the string, including spaces.

substr_count($str, ' ') counts the number of spaces in the string.

Subtracting the number of spaces from the total length gives the count of characters without spaces.

**echo ("Total ".$char." characters
");**

Here, it prints the total count of characters in the string (excluding spaces) by concatenating the variable $char with a message.

$words = str_word_count($str);

This code uses the str_word_count() function to count the number of words in the string. The function considers a "word" as a sequence of characters separated by spaces.

**echo ("Total ".$words." words
");**

Finally, it prints the total count of words in the string by concatenating the variable $words with a message.

In this example, the code successfully calculates and displays the total number of characters (excluding spaces) and the total number of words in the given string.

18. A 9x9 multiplication table

Source Code 18

```php
<?php
for($i=1;$i<=9;$i++){
echo "<br>";
for($j=1;$j<=$i;$j++){
echo "{$i}x{$j}=".($i*$j)." ";
}}
```

Output:

1*1= 1

2*1= 2 2*2= 4

3*1= 3 3*2= 6 3*3= 9

4*1= 4 4*2= 8 4*3=12 4*4=16

5*1= 5 5*2=10 5*3=15 5*4=20 5*5=25

6*1= 6 6*2=12 6*3=18 6*4=24 6*5=30 6*6=36

7*1= 7 7*2=14 7*3=21 7*4=28 7*5=35 7*6=42 7*7=49

8*1= 8 8*2=16 8*3=24 8*4=32 8*5=40 8*6=48 8*7=56 8*8=64

9*1= 9 9*2=18 9*3=27 9*4=36 9*5=45 9*6=54 9*7=63 9*8=72 9*9=81

This PHP code generates a multiplication table for numbers from 1 to 9. It uses nested for loops to iterate through each number and print the products of multiplication.

Let's break down the code step by step:

for ($i = 1; $i <= 9; $i++) {

This is the outer for loop, which iterates from 1 to 9 (inclusive). It controls the row of the multiplication table.

echo "<br>";

Inside the outer loop, this code adds a line break (<br>) to start a new row in the multiplication table.

for ($j = 1; $j <= $i; $j++) {

This is the inner for loop. It iterates from 1 to the current value of $i. It controls the columns in the multiplication table and ensures that only the products for the numbers up to $i are displayed in each row.

echo "{$i}x{$j}=" . ($i * $j) . " ";

Inside the inner loop, this code prints the multiplication expression and its result. For example, if $i is 3 and $j is 2, it will print "3x2=6 ".

"{$i}" is replaced with the current value of the variable $i.

"x" is a literal character 'x'.

"{$j}" is replaced with the current value of the variable $j.

"{$i}x{$j}" will be a string like "1x1", "2x1", "2x2", "3x1", "3x2", "3x3", and so on, depending on the values of $i and $j in each iteration of the nested loops.

"($i*$j)" calculates the product of the current values of $i and $j.

For example, if $i is 2 and $j is 3, then "($i*$j)" will be evaluated as (2 * 3), resulting in 6.

In summary, this code generates a simple multiplication table with rows and columns, displaying the products of numbers from 1 to 9.

19. The greatest common divisor

Source Code 19

```php
<?php
$x = 20;
$y = 30;
if ($x > $y) {
  $temp = $x;
  $x = $y;
  $y = $temp;
}
for($n = 1; $n < ($x+1); $n++) {
  if ($x%$n == 0 and $y%$n == 0)
    $gcd = $n;
}
echo "The greatest common divisor is: $gcd";
?>
```

The greatest common divisor is: 10

This PHP code calculates the greatest common divisor (GCD) of two numbers, $x and $y, using a straightforward method and then prints the result.

Let's break down each part of the code:

$x = 20; $y = 30;

These lines initialize two variables, $x and $y, with the values 20 and 30, respectively. These are the two numbers for which we want to find the GCD.

if ($x > $y) {

$temp = $x; $x = $y; $y = $temp;

}

This code snippet is used to ensure that $x holds the smaller of the two numbers and $y holds the larger one. If $x is greater than $y, it swaps the values of $x and $y using a temporary variable $temp. This step ensures that the subsequent GCD calculation is performed correctly.

for($n = 1; $n < ($x+1); $n++) {

This line starts a for loop. It initializes a variable $n to 1, runs the loop as long as $n is less than $x+1, and increments $n in each iteration.

if ($x%$n == 0 and $y%$n == 0)

$gcd = $n;

Inside the loop, this line checks if both $x and $y are divisible by the current value of $n without a remainder. If true, it updates the variable $gcd to the current value of $n. This is done to find the greatest common divisor (GCD) of $x and $y.

echo "The greatest common divisor is: $gcd";

Finally, this code prints the calculated GCD, which is stored in the $gcd variable, as a part of a message.

So, the greatest common divisor of 20 and 30 is 10. The code correctly calculates and displays this result.

In summary, this PHP program calculates the greatest common divisor (GCD) of two numbers, $x and $y, using the Euclidean algorithm.

20. The least common multiple

```php
<?php
$x = 20;
$y = 30;
if ($x > $y) {
  $temp = $x;
  $x = $y;
  $y = $temp;
}
for($n = 1; $n < ($x+1); $n++) {
  if ($x%$n == 0 && $y%$n == 0)
    $gcd = $n;
}
$lcm = ($x*$y)/$gcd;
echo "The least common multiply is: $lcm";
?>
```

Output:

The least common multiply is: 60

Explanation:

This PHP code calculates the least common multiple (LCM) of two numbers, $a and $b, using their greatest common divisor (GCD) and then prints the result. It's a common approach to find the LCM when we know the GCD of two numbers.

$x = 20; $y = 30;

These lines initialize two variables, $x and $y, with the values 20 and 30, respectively. These are the two numbers for which we want to find the LCM.

if ($x > $y) {

$temp = $x; $x = $y; $y = $temp;

}

This code snippet is used to ensure that $x holds the smaller of the two numbers and $y holds the larger one. If $x is greater than $y, it swaps the values of $x and $y using a temporary variable $temp. This step ensures that the subsequent GCD and LCM calculations are performed correctly.

for($n = 1; $n < ($x+1); $n++) {

This line starts a for loop. It initializes a variable $n to 1, runs the loop as long as $n is less than $x+1, and increments $n in each iteration.

if ($x%$n == 0 && $y%$n == 0)

$gcd = $n;

Inside the loop, this line checks if both $x and $y are divisible by the current value of $n without a remainder. If true, it updates the variable $gcd to the current value of $n. This is done to find the greatest common divisor (GCD) of $x and $y.

$lcm = ($x * $y) / $gcd;

After finding the GCD, this code calculates the LCM using the formula: LCM = (a * b) / GCD

It multiplies $x and $y and then divides the result by the calculated GCD to obtain the LCM.

echo "The least common multiply is: $lcm";

Finally, this code prints the calculated LCM, which is stored in the $lcm variable, as a part of a message. The code correctly calculates and displays this result based on the provided GCD and LCM formula.

In summary, this PHP program calculates the least common multiple (LCM) of two numbers, $x and $y, using the formula LCM = (x * y) / GCD. It first ensures that $x contains the smaller value, then finds the GCD using a loop, and finally calculates and prints the LCM.

21. Login page

```
<!DOCTYPE html>

<html>

<body>

Assume the username: ray,  password: 12345

<br>

<form method="post" action="Sign.php"><br>

UserName: <input type="text" name="user"><br>

<br>

PassWord: <input type="password" name="pass"><br>

<br>

<input type="submit" value="Sign in">

</form>

</body>

</html>
```

Output:

Assume the username: ray, password: 12345

UserName: [   ]

PassWord: [   ]

[Sign in]

(Sign.php)

```php
<!DOCTYPE html>

<html>

<body>

<?php

$user = $_POST['user'];

$pass = $_POST['pass'];

if($user == 'ray' and $pass == '12345'){

    echo "Signed in successfully";

}

?>

</body>

</html>
```

Output:

Signed in successfully

1. Form.php:

**<!DOCTYPE html> <html> <body> Assume the username: ray, password: 12345
 ……**

This HTML file sets up a basic web page. It displays some text to inform the user about assumed credentials (username: ray, password: 12345).

It contains a <form> element with the following attributes:

method="post": Specifies that the form data should be sent to the server using the HTTP POST method, which is suitable for handling sensitive information like passwords.

action="Sign.php": Specifies that when the form is submitted, the data should be sent to the "Sign.php" script for processing.

**UserName: <input type="text" name="user">
**

This code displays the label "UserName" and an input field. The name attribute of the input field is set to "user." This name will be used to identify the input field when the form is submitted.

**PassWord: <input type="password" name="pass">
**

Similar to the previous line, this one displays the label "PassWord" and an input field for the password. The type attribute is set to "password," which hides the entered characters as dots or asterisks for security reasons.

<input type="submit" value="Sign in">

This code adds a submit button with the label "Sign in." When the user clicks this button, the form data will be sent to the "Sign.php" script for processing.

</form> </body> </html>

This closes the HTML form and the web page.

2. Sign.php:

<?php

$user = $_POST['user'];

$pass = $_POST['pass'];

This begins by opening PHP tags (<?php) to start the PHP code.

The PHP code retrieves the values of the "user" and "pass" fields submitted through the HTML form using the $_POST superglobal. It assigns these values to the variables $user and $pass.

if($user == 'ray' and $pass == '12345'){

echo "Signed in successfully";

}

?>

This PHP code checks if the values of $user and $pass match the assumed username and password (ray and 12345) using an if statement. If they match, it displays "Signed in successfully."

"?>" ends the PHP code.

22. Select our favorite car

```html
<html>
 <body>
  <form action="Car.php" method="post">
   <b>Please enter your favorite car:</b>
   <br>
   <input type="text" size="40" name="car"><br><br>
   <b>Please select your favorite color :</b> <br>
   <input type="radio" name="color" value="golden">  Golden
   <input type="radio" name="color" value="silver">  Silver
   <input type="radio" name="color" value="purple">    Blue
   <br><br>
   <input type="submit" value="Submit Your Favorite.">
  </form>
 </body>
</html>
```

Output:

Please enter your favorite car:

Please select your favorite color:

○ Golden ○ Silver ○ Blue

Submit Your Favorite.

(Car.php)

```
<html>
 <body>
 <?php
  $color = $_POST['color'];
  $car = $_POST['car'];
  if(( $color != null ) && ( $car != null )){
        $data = "Your favorite car is $car <br>";
        $data .= "and with color of $color ";
  }
  echo $data;
 ?>
</body>
</html>
```

Output:

Your favorite car is Cool Car
and with color of golden

1. Form.php:

<form action="Car.php" method="post">

**<b>Please enter your favorite car:</b>
**

**<input type="text" size="40" name="car">

**

This HTML file sets up a web page with a form. The form's action attribute is set to "Car.php," which means that when the form is submitted, the data will be sent to the "Car.php" script for processing.

It contains a text input field for users to enter their favorite car. The name attribute is set to "car" so that we can reference this input field in the PHP script. The <b> tags are used for bold text.

**Please select your favorite color :</b>
**

<input type="radio" name="color" value="golden"> Golden

<input type="radio" name="color" value="silver"> Silver

<input type="radio" name="color" value="purple"> Blue

This part of the form asks users to select their favorite color using radio buttons. The name attribute is set to "color," and each radio button has a different value.

The labels for the radio buttons are "Golden," "Silver," and "Blue."

<input type="submit" value="Submit Your Favorite.">

</form> </body> </html>

This section adds a submit button to the form with the label "Submit Your Favorite." When the user clicks this button, the form data will be sent to "Car.php" for processing.

The HTML tags are closed to end the web page.

2. Car.php:

```php
<?php

$color = $_POST['color']; $car = $_POST['car'];
```

This begins by opening PHP tags (<?php) to start the PHP code.

The PHP code retrieves the values of the "color" and "car" fields submitted through the HTML form using the $_POST superglobal. It assigns these values to the variables $color and $car.

```php
if(($color != null) && ($car != null)){

$data = "Your favorite car is $car <br>";

$data .= "and with the color of $color ";

}

echo $data;

?>
```

The PHP code checks if both $color and $car are not null (i.e., if the user has entered values for both fields). If both values are provided, it constructs a message stored in the $data variable, which includes the user's favorite car and color.

Finally, the PHP code uses echo to display the message stored in the $data variable. "?>" ends the PHP code.

23. A simple calculator

Source Code 23　(Form.php)

```
<html>
 <body>
  <form action = "Calculate.php" method = "post"><br>
  Number 1: <input type = "text" name = "data1" size =
"8"><br><br>
   Number 2: <input type = "text" name = "data2" size =
"8"><br><br>
  <input type = "radio" name = "operator" value = "a"> Add
  <input type = "radio" name = "operator" value = "s"> Sub
  <input type = "radio" name = "operator" value = "m"> Mul
  <input type = "radio" name = "operator" value = "d"> Div
  <br><br>
  <input type = "submit" value = "Submit">
  <input type = "reset" value = "Reset">
  </form>
 </body>
</html>
```

Output:

Number 1: `100`

Number 2: `2`

○ Add   ○ Sub   ⊙ Mul   ○ Div

[Submit] [Reset]

(Calculate.php)

```php
<html><body>
<?php
 $data1 = $_POST['data1'];
 $data2 = $_POST['data2'];
 $operator = $_POST['operator'];
   if( is_numeric( $data1 ) && is_numeric( $data2 ) ){
      if( $operator != null ){
      switch( $operator ){
      case "a" : $outcome = $data1 + $data2; break;
      case "s" : $outcome = $data1 - $data2; break;
      case "m" : $outcome = $data1 * $data2; break;
      case "d" : $outcome = $data1 / $data2; break;
      }
      echo( "The result is: $outcome" );
   }}
   else{ echo( "Input error! Please try again" ); }
?>
</body></html>
```

(Assume that 100 X 2)

The result is: 200

Explanation:

1. Form.php:

<form action="Calculate.php" method="post">

action: Specifies the URL to which the form data will be sent when the form is submitted and it's set to "Calculate.php".

method: Specifies the HTTP method to be used when sending form data. In this case, it's set to "post".

Number 1: <input type="text" name="data1" size="8">

Number 2: <input type="text" name="data2" size="8">

These lines create two text input fields labeled "Number 1" and "Number 2". Users can input numerical values in these fields. The name attribute is used to identify these fields when the form is submitted.

<input type="radio" name="operator" value="a"> Add......

These lines create a set of radio buttons for selecting an arithmetic operation. Each radio button has a value attribute representing the operation ("a" for addition, "s" for subtraction, "m" for multiplication, and "d" for division). The name attribute is used to group the radio buttons.

```html
<input type="submit" value="Submit">
```

```html
<input type="reset" value="Reset">
```

These lines create two buttons: a submit button and a reset button. The submit button, when clicked, will submit the form data to the URL specified in the action attribute. The reset button will clear the input

2. Calculate.php:

```php
$data1 = $_POST['data1'];
```

```php
$data2 = $_POST['data2'];
```

```php
$operator = $_POST['operator'];
```

These lines retrieve the user input from the HTML form. The $_POST superglobal is used to collect form data sent with the HTTP POST method.

```php
if (is_numeric($data1) && is_numeric($data2)) {
```

This conditional statement checks if both $data1 and $data2 are numeric using the is_numeric function. It ensures that the user has entered valid numerical values.

```php
if ($operator != null) {
  switch ($operator) {
    case "a": $outcome = $data1 + $data2; break;
    case "s": $outcome = $data1 - $data2; break;
    case "m": $outcome = $data1 * $data2; break;
```

```
        case "d": $outcome = $data1 / $data2; break;

    }

    echo("The result is: $outcome");

}
```

If the user has selected an operator ($operator is not null), a switch statement is used to perform the corresponding arithmetic operation based on the value of $operator. The result is stored in the $outcome variable.

echo("The result is: $outcome");

The result of the arithmetic operation is echoed and displayed on the webpage.

} else { echo("Input error! Please try again"); }

If the input validation fails (i.e., if either $data1 or $data2 is not numeric), an error message is echoed and displayed on the webpage.

In summary, this PHP script takes user input from an HTML form, performs an arithmetic operation based on the selected operator, and displays the result or an error message depending on the input validity.

24. Count how many persons visiting us

Source Code 24   (Web.php)

```php
<?php
$fp = fopen ("Visitors.txt","r+");
$counter = fgets ($fp,80);
$counter = doubleval ($counter) + 1;
fseek ($fp,0);
fputs ($fp,$counter);
fclose ($fp);
?>
<html>
<body>
<br><br>
<center>
Total <strong><?php echo $counter?></strong> persons visited us<br>
</center>
</body>
</html>
```

(Please open and refresh the web page)

(Visitors.txt)

```
1
```

Output:

Total **168** persons visited us

Explanation:

Web.php:

<?php $fp = fopen("Visitors.txt", "r+");

This code opens the file "Visitors.txt" for reading and writing ("r+" mode) and assigns the file resource to the variable $fp. This file is used to store the visitor count.

$counter = fgets($fp, 80);

The fgets function is used to read a line from the opened file. It reads up to 80 characters from the file and assigns the value to the variable $counter. In this case, it reads the number "1" from "Visitors.txt," which represents the current visitor count.

$counter = doubleval($counter) + 1;

The value read from the file is converted to a floating-point number using the doubleval function. This step is necessary to ensure that the count can be incremented. Then, it adds 1 to the current count, effectively incrementing it by 1.

fseek($fp, 0);

The fseek function is used to move the file pointer back to the beginning of the file. This is necessary to overwrite the existing count with the updated count.

fputs($fp, $counter);

The fputs function (which is similar to fwrite) is used to write the updated count ($counter) back to the file. This effectively updates the visitor count in "Visitors.txt."

fclose($fp);

Finally, the file is closed using fclose to free up system resources.

<center>

**Total <?php echo $counter?> persons visited us
**

</center>

The HTML section of the file displays the visitor count to the user. It uses PHP to embed the value of $counter into the HTML, displaying the total number of visitors.

In summary, "Web.php" is a PHP script that opens a text file ("Visitors.txt") to read and update the visitor count. It then displays the updated count to the user on an HTML page. Each time someone accesses the web page, the visitor count in "Visitors.txt" is incremented by 1, and the updated count is displayed on the page.

25. Select a website to visit

Source Code 25

```php
<?php

    $website = $_POST['website'];

    $self = $_SERVER['PHP_SELF'];

    if( $website != null ){

      header( "Location:$website") ;

      exit();

    }
?>
<html>
 <body>
  <p> </p>
  <p> </p>
  <p align="center">Please select a website to visit:  </p>
  <form action = "<?php $self ?>" method = "post">
    <div align="center">
      <select name = "website">
       <option value =
      "http://www.amazon.com/author/ray-yao">RAY</option>
        <option value = "http://www.cnn.com">CNN</option>
```

```
        <option value = "http://www.bbc.com">BBC</option>

        <option value = "http://www.abc.com">ABC</option>

        <option value = "http://www.foxnews.com">FOX</option>

      </select>

    <input type = "submit" value = "Click Here!">

    </div>

  </form>

</body>

</html>
```

Output:

Please select a website to visit:

Explanation:

This code is an example of a simple PHP script that allows users to select a website from a dropdown menu and then redirects them to the selected website. Here's a breakdown of the code:

<?php and ?>: These are PHP tags that enclose the PHP code. This signifies the beginning and end of the PHP code block.

$website = $_POST['website'];: This code retrieves the value of the "website" field from the HTTP POST request data and assigns it to the $website variable. This variable will store the URL of the website the user selects from the dropdown menu.

$self = $_SERVER['PHP_SELF'];: Here, the $_SERVER superglobal is used to get the current script's filename (in this case, $_SERVER['PHP_SELF'] represents the filename of the current script) and stores it in the $self variable.

if ($website != null) { ... }: This is an if statement that checks if the $website variable is not null, meaning the user has selected a website from the dropdown.

header("Location:$website");: If the user has selected a website, this code uses the header() function to send an HTTP redirect header to the URL specified in the $website variable. This will instruct the browser to navigate to the selected website.

exit();: After sending the redirect header, the exit() function is called to terminate the script execution, ensuring that no further HTML or PHP code is processed.

<form action="<?php $self ?>" method="post">

This line starts a form with the following attributes:

action: Specifies the URL to which the form data will be sent when the form is submitted. However, there's an issue with the PHP code inside the attribute (<?php $self ?>). It seems like it's attempting to use a PHP variable called $self, but it's not correctly capturing the current script's URL. It should be <?php echo $_SERVER['PHP_SELF']; ?> to get the correct URL.

method = "post": Specifies the HTTP method to be used when sending form data. In this case, it's set to "post", which is used to send data to the server as part of the HTTP request body.

(method="get": Specifies the HTTP method to be used when sending form data, but the code is used to append form data to the URL as query parameters.)

<select name="website"> …… </select>

This creates a dropdown (select) menu with the name "website." Each <option> represents a different website with a corresponding URL.

<input type="submit" value="Click Here!">

This line creates a submit button with the text "Click Here!".

This form allows users to select a website from a dropdown menu and, upon clicking the "Click Here!" button, the form data will be submitted to the same script. Note that the action attribute needs correction to <?php echo $_SERVER['PHP_SELF']; ?> to capture the correct script URL.

In summary, this PHP script displays a webpage with a dropdown menu of website options. When a user selects a website and clicks the "Click Here!" button, the PHP code redirects them to the selected website using the header("Location: $website"); function.

26. Upload a photo

Source Code 26

```php
<?php
echo <<<_END
<form method="post"  action="$_SERVER[PHP_SELF]"
    enctype="multipart/form-data">
<input  type="hidden"  name="flag" value="1" />
<input  type="file"    name="photo" />
<input  type="submit" value="Upload" /></form>
_END;
if (isset($_POST['flag'])){
  $result = PIPHP_UploadFile("photo",
    array("image/jpeg", "image/pjpeg"), 100000);
  if ($result[0] == 0){
    file_put_contents("photo.jpg", $result[2]);
    echo "Photo is uploaded successfully!<br />";
    echo "Please check the uploaded photo: <a
href='photo.jpg'>photo.jpg</a><br />";
  }
  else{
    if ($result[0] == -2) echo "Wrong file type<br />";
    if ($result[0] == -3) echo "Maximum length exceeded<br />";
```

```php
        if ($result[0] > 0)   echo "Error code: $result<br />";

        echo "File upload failed<br />";

 }}
function PIPHP_UploadFile($name, $filetypes, $maxlen){

  if (!isset($_FILES[$name]['name']))

    return array(-1, NULL, NULL);

  if (!in_array($_FILES[$name]['type'], $filetypes))

    return array(-2, NULL, NULL);

  if ($_FILES[$name]['size'] > $maxlen)

    return array(-3, NULL, NULL);

  if ($_FILES[$name]['error'] > 0)

    return array($_FILES[$name]['error'], NULL, NULL);

  $temp = file_get_contents($_FILES[$name]['tmp_name']);

  return array(0, $_FILES[$name]['type'], $temp);

}
?>
```

(Assume that we uploaded a photo named "photo.jpg")

Photo is uploaded successfully!

Please check the uploaded photo: photo.jpg

Explanation:

echo <<<_END: This is the heredoc syntax, used to output a multi-line string. The string begins with _END and ends with **_END;.** Everything between these markers is treated as a string and is immediately echoed to the output.

Inside the heredoc block, there's an HTML form that allows the user to upload a file. Here's what each part of the form does:

**<form method="post" action="$_SERVER[PHP_SELF]"** enctype="multipart/form-data">: This <form> element specifies that the form will be submitted using the HTTP POST method (method="post") to the current script (action = "$_SERVER [PHP_SELF]"). The enctype attribute is set to "multipart/form-data," which is required when uploading files.

<input type="hidden" name="flag" value="1" />: This hidden input field with the name "flag" is used to indicate that the form has been submitted. It's given a fixed value of "1."

<input type="file" name="photo" />: This input field of type "file" allows the user to select a file for uploading. The name attribute is "photo," which will be used to reference the file in the PHP code.

<input type="submit" value="Upload" />: This is a submit button for the form.

**if (isset($_POST['flag'])){ :** isset($_POST['flag']) checks if the form is submitted. The form seems to contain a field with the name "flag," and this condition ensures that the script executes when the form is submitted.

$result = PIPHP_UploadFile("photo", array("image/jpeg", "image/pjpeg"), 100000); : Call to PIPHP_UploadFile Function, the code is calling a custom function named PIPHP_UploadFile. This function is handling the file upload process. It is passing three parameters to the function:

"photo": The name of the file input field in the form.

array("image/jpeg", "image/pjpeg"): An array of allowed file types (JPEG images in this case).

100000: Maximum file size in bytes (100,000 bytes or approximately 100 KB).

if ($result[0] == 0){: Check the Result of File Upload, $result[0] is the first element of the array returned by PIPHP_UploadFile. It checks if the file upload was successful (result code 0).

file_put_contents("photo.jpg", $result[2]);: Handle Successful File Upload, If the file upload is successful ($result[0] == 0), it uses file_put_contents to save the uploaded file as "photo.jpg."

It then outputs success messages with a link to the uploaded photo.

**if ($result[0] == -2) echo "Wrong file type
";**
**if ($result[0] == -3) echo "Maximum length exceeded
";**
**if ($result[0] > 0)   echo "Error code: $result
";**
**echo "File upload failed
";**

These codes Handle File Upload Errors, if the file upload is not successful, it checks the error code and outputs corresponding error messages. Common error codes include:

-2: Wrong file type. -3: Maximum length exceeded. > 0: Errors

function PIPHP_UploadFile($name, $filetypes, $maxlen){: This line declares a function named PIPHP_UploadFile with three parameters: $name, $filetypes, and $maxlen. These parameters

288

represent the name of the file input field, an array of allowed file types, and the maximum allowed file size, respectively.

if (!isset($_FILES[$name]['name'])): This code checks if the file name is set in the $_FILES array. If not, it returns an array with the result code -1 and two NULL values.

if (!in_array($_FILES[$name]['type'], $filetypes)): This code checks if the file type is in the allowed types specified by the $filetypes parameter. If not, it returns an array with the result code -2 and two NULL values.

if ($_FILES[$name]['size'] > $maxlen): This code checks if the file size exceeds the maximum allowed size specified by the $maxlen parameter. If it does, it returns an array with the result code -3 and two NULL values.

if ($_FILES[$name]['error'] > 0): This code checks if there was an error during the file upload process. If there was, it returns an array with the error code and two NULL values.

$temp = file_get_contents($_FILES[$name]['tmp_name']);

return array(0, $_FILES[$name]['type'], $temp);

These codes read and return file contents on success, if all the checks pass, it reads the contents of the temporary file ($_FILES[$name]['tmp_name']) using file_get_contents and returns an array with the result code 0, the file type, and the file contents.

27. Words processing

```
<html>
<head>
<style type="type="text/css">
<!--
.STYLE1 {
        font-family: Arial, Helvetica, sans-serif;
        font-weight: bold;
        font-size: 16px;
}
-->
</style>
</head>
 <body>
 <form action="<?php echo( $self ); ?>" method="post">
 <class="STYLE1">Please input some sentences below: <br>
 <textarea name="words" rows="3" cols="60" ></textarea><br>
  <p class="STYLE1">Please select one option below: <br>
  <input type="radio" name="process" value="strtoupper">
  Alter the sentence to uppercase<br>
   <input type="radio" name="process" value="strtolower">
```

Alter the sentence to lowercase\

\<input type="radio" name="process" value="ucwords">

Alter the first letter to uppercase\

\<input type="radio" name="process" value="strlen">

Check the length of the sentence\

\<input type="radio" name="process" value="strrev">

Make the sentence reversed\
\
 \</p>

\<input type="submit" value="Process">

\</form>

\<?php

$words = $_POST['words'];

$process = $_POST['process'];

echo $words."\
";

echo $process($words);

?>

\</body>

\</html>

Output:

Please input some sentences below:

```
PHP is very good
```

Please select one option below:

⊙ Alter the sentence to uppercase

○ Alter the sentence to lowercase

○ Alter the first letter to uppercase

○ Check the length of the sentence

○ Make the sentence reversed

[Process]

PHP is very good
PHP IS VERY GOOD

Explanation:

.STYLE1{ }: This is a CSS class selector. It targets HTML elements with the class attribute set to "STYLE1." The dot (.) before the class name indicates that it is a class selector.

The curly braces enclose the style rules that apply to elements with the class "STYLE1."

<form>: This tag defines the beginning of an HTML form.

action="<?php echo($self); ?>": The action attribute specifies the URL to which the form data will be submitted. In this case, it uses PHP to echo the value of the variable $self, which is expected to represent the current script or URL.

method="post": The method attribute specifies the HTTP method used to send form data. Here, it's set to "post," meaning the form data will be sent as part of the HTTP request body.

(method="get": Append form data to the URL as parameters.)

<textarea>: This tag defines a multi-line text input area.

name="words": The name attribute specifies the name of the form field, which will be used to identify this field when the form is submitted.

rows="3" and cols="60": These attributes set the number of visible rows and columns in the textarea.

<input type="radio">: These tags define radio buttons for selecting processing options.

name="process": The name attribute groups the radio buttons together, allowing the user to choose only one option.

value: The value attribute specifies the value that will be sent to the server when the form is submitted.

The options include altering the sentence to uppercase, lowercase, title case, checking the length, and reversing the sentence.

<input type="submit">: This tag defines a submit button.

The button is labeled "Process," and clicking it will submit the form data to the URL specified in the action attribute.

$words = $_POST['words'];: This line retrieves the value submitted for the form field with the name "words" using the $_POST superglobal. It assigns the value to the variable $words.

$process = $_POST['process'];: This line retrieves the value submitted for the radio button group with the name "process" using the $_POST superglobal. It assigns the value to the variable $process.

**echo $words."
";:** This line outputs the submitted sentence ($words) followed by a line break (<br>) to display it on the web page.

echo $process($words);: This line invokes a function based on the value of the $process variable. It passes the submitted sentence ($words) as an argument to the function.

The exact function that is called depends on the value submitted for the radio button group named "process."

This program processes the form data submitted from the HTML form. The PHP code retrieves the submitted sentence and the selected processing option. It then displays the submitted sentence and invokes a processing function based on the selected option, displaying the result on the web page. The actual processing functions (e.g., strtoupper, strtolower, etc.) are expected to be predefined functions in PHP or functions we have defined elsewhere in our code.

28. Using session

Source Code 28   (File1.php)

```php
<?php

session_start();

?>

<html>

<body>

<br>

<?php

$_SESSION["id"] = "Ray Yao";

echo "Session is applied successfully!<br/>";

?>

<br>

<a href="file2.php">Click here to see more information</a>

</body>

</html>
```

Output:

Session is applied successfully!

Click here to see more information

```php
<?php
session_start();
?>
<html>
<body>
<?php
echo "Hello! I am ".$_SESSION["id"]."<br>";
echo "The session comes to here finally!"
?>
</body>
</html>
```

Output:

Hello! I am Ray Yao

The session comes to here finally!

Explanation:

1. File1.php:

session_start();: This function is called at the beginning of the script to start a new or resume an existing session. It's required for working with sessions in PHP.

$_SESSION["id"] = "Ray Yao";: In this code, the user's name, "Ray Yao," is stored in the session variable $_SESSION["id"]. This data will persist across multiple pages during the same session.

**echo "Session is applied successfully!
";:** A message is displayed to confirm that the session has been successfully initialized and the user's data has been stored.

<a href="file2.php">Click here to see more information</a>: A link is provided to File2.php, allowing the user to navigate to the second page and retrieve the session data.

2. File2.php:

session_start();: Just like in File1.php, this function is called to start or resume the session.

**echo "Hello! I am ".$_SESSION["id"]."
";:** This code retrieves the user's name, which was stored in the session on the previous page (in $_SESSION["id"]), and displays it along with a greeting.

echo "The session comes to here finally!": A message is displayed to indicate that the session has continued and reached this point in the second file.

Here's how the session flow works between these two files:

In File1.php, the session is started, and the user's name "Ray Yao" is stored in the $_SESSION["id"] variable.

The user is provided with a link to navigate to File2.php.

When the user clicks the link and goes to File2.php, the session is resumed using session_start().

In File2.php, the user's name ("Ray Yao") is retrieved from the $_SESSION["id"] variable and displayed on the page.

A message is displayed in File2.php to indicate that the session data has been successfully passed from File1.php to File2.php.

This is a simple demonstration of how PHP sessions can be used to maintain user data and state across multiple web pages. Sessions are particularly useful for maintaining user login status, shopping cart contents, and other persistent data throughout a user's visit to a website.

29. Using cookie

```php
<?php

    $username =  $_POST['username'];

    $language = $_POST['language'];

    $self =  $_SERVER['PHP_SELF'];

    if( ( $username != null ) and ( $language != null ) ){

      setcookie( "username", $username , time() + 36000 );

      setcookie( "language", $language, time() + 36000 );

      header( "Location:file2.php" );

      exit();

    }
?>
<html>
<body>
 <form action ="<?php echo( $self ); ?>" method = "post">
 Please enter your user name:
 <input type = "text" name = "username">
 <br>
  <br>
 Please choose your favorite programming language:<br>
```

```
<input type = "radio" name = "language" value = "JAVA">JAVA

<input type = "radio" name = "language" value = "RUBY">RUBY

<input type = "radio" name = "language" value = "HTML">HTML

<br>

<br>

<input type = "submit" value = "submit">

</form>

</body>

</html>
```

Output:

Please enter your user name: | Ray Yao |

Please choose your favorite programming language:

◉ JAVA ○ RUBY ○ HTML

| submit |

(File2.php)

```php
<?php

        $username  = $_COOKIE['username'];

        $language = $_COOKIE['language'];

?>

<html>

 <head>

   <style type = "text/css">

   body { language: <?php echo( $language ); ?> }

  </style>

 </head>

 <body>

  <h3>Hi, <?php echo( $username ); ?>! </h3>

  <h3>Your favorite language is:  <?php echo( $language ); ?>

  </h3>

 </body></html>
```

Output:

Hi, Ray Yao!
Your favorite language is: JAVA

Explanation:

1. File1.php:

$username = $_POST['username'];: This line retrieves the value submitted for the form field with the name "username" using the $_POST superglobal. It assigns the value to the variable $username.

$language = $_POST['language'];: This line retrieves the value submitted for the form field with the name "language" using the $_POST superglobal. It assigns the value to the $language.

$self = $_SERVER['PHP_SELF'];: This line retrieves the current script filename (including its path) using $_SERVER['PHP_SELF'] and assigns it to the variable $self. This information is often used for redirecting after form submission.

if(($username != null) and ($language != null)){: This line checks if both $username and $language have non-null values. The condition ($username != null) and ($language != null) ensures that both fields are filled in the form.

setcookie("username", $username, time() + 36000);: This line sets a cookie named "username" with the value of $username. The cookie is set to expire in 36000 seconds (10 hours) from the current time.

setcookie("language", $language, time() + 36000);: Similarly, this line sets a cookie named "language" with the value of $language. The cookie is set to expire in 36000 seconds (10 hours) from the current time.

header("Location:file2.php");: This line sends an HTTP header to the browser, instructing it to redirect to the specified location (in this case, "file2.php").

exit();: The exit() function is then called to terminate the script immediately. This is important after sending a location header to ensure that no further code is executed.

<form>: This is the opening tag for an HTML form. It is used to create a form that will be submitted.

action ="<?php echo($self); ?>": The action attribute specifies the URL or script to which the form data will be submitted. In this case, it uses PHP to dynamically set the form action to the current script ($self represents the script file).

method = "post": The method attribute specifies the HTTP method used to send form data to the server. In this case, it's set to "post," indicating that data will be sent as part of the HTTP request body.

<input type = "text" name = "username">: This creates a text input field with the name attribute set to "username." The value entered by the user will be sent to the server with this name.

<input type = "radio" name = "language" value = "JAVA"> JAVA: This creates a radio button with the name attribute set to "language" and the value attribute set to "JAVA." Users can choose only one option from these radio buttons.

Similar radio buttons are created for "RUBY" and "HTML."

<input type = "submit" value = "submit">: This creates a submit button. When clicked, it will submit the form data to the URL specified in the action attribute.

</form>: This is the closing tag for the HTML form.

2. File2.php:

$username = $_COOKIE['username'];: This line retrieves the value of the cookie named "username" using the $_COOKIE superglobal. The value is assigned to the variable $username. Cookies are used to store information on the client side, and in this case, the script is retrieving the previously set username cookie.

$language = $_COOKIE['language'];: Similarly, this line retrieves the value of the cookie named "language" and assigns it to the variable $language.

This PHP code is used to retrieve values from cookies. The variables $username and $language will now contain the values stored in the "username" and "language" cookies, respectively. These values could have been set in a previous script using the setcookie function or some other mechanism. The cookies typically store information that persists across multiple requests, allowing the server to remember information about the client.

30. Create a MySQL database using PHP

Source Code 30

```php
<?php
// Database connection parameters
$servername = "your_servername";
// Substitute with your database server name or IP address
$username = "your_username";
// Substitute with your MySQL username
$password = "your_password";
// Substitute with your MySQL password
// Create a connection to MySQL
$con = new mysqli($servername, $username, $password);
if ($con->connect_error) {    // Check connection
    die("Connection failed: " . $con->connect_error);
}
// SQL query to create a new database
$dbname = "your_database";
// Substitute with the desired database name
$sql = "CREATE DATABASE $dbname";
// Execute the query
if ($con->query($sql) === TRUE) {
```

```php
    echo "Database created successfully";

} else {

    echo "Error creating database: " . $con->error;

}

// Close the database connection

$con->close();

?>
```

Explanation:

$servername, $username, and $password: These variables store the server name, username, and password needed to connect to the MySQL server. We should replace "your_servername," "your_username," and "your_password" with our actual MySQL server details.

$con = new mysqli($servername, $username, $password);: This line creates a new MySQLi (MySQL Improved) object named $con for database connection using the provided server name, username, and password.

if ($con->connect_error) {: This checks if the connection to the MySQL server was unsuccessful.

die("Connection failed: " . $con->connect_error);: If the connection fails, the script terminates and outputs an error message.

$dbname = "your_database";: This variable stores the name of the database we want to create. We should replace "your_database" with our desired database name.

$sql = "CREATE DATABASE $dbname";: This SQL query string creates a database with the name stored in the $dbname variable.

if ($con->query($sql) === TRUE) {: This line executes the SQL query using the query method of the MySQLi object ($con). If the query is successful, it proceeds to the next block of code.

echo "Database created successfully";: If the database creation is successful, this message is echoed.

} else {: If the query fails, this block of code is executed.

echo "Error creating database: " . $con->error;: This line outputs an **error message, including details about the error.**

$con->close();: This line closes the database connection. It's good practice to close the connection once it's no longer needed.

In summary, this PHP script connects to a MySQL server, creates a new database with the specified name, and outputs success or error messages. Ensure that we replace placeholder values (server name, username, password, and database name) with our actual MySQL server details and preferences.

31. Connect to a MySQL server using PHP

Source Code 31   (connect.php)

```php
<?php

$servername = "your_servername";

$username = "your_username";

$password = "your_password";

$dbname = "your_dbname";

// Create a connection to the MySQL server

$con = new mysqli($servername, $username, $password,
$dbname);

// Check the connection

if ($con->connect_error) {

    die("Connection failed: " . $con->connect_error);

}

echo "Connected successfully";

// Close the database connection when done

$con->close();

?>
```

(File name: **connect.php**)

Explanation:

$servername, $username, $password: These variables store the server name, username, and password needed to connect to the MySQL server. We should replace "your_servername," "your_username," and "your_password" with our actual MySQL server details.

$dbname: This variable stores the name of the database to which we want to connect. Replace "your_dbname" with the actual name of our database.

$con = new mysqli($servername, $username, $password, $dbname);: This line creates a new MySQLi (MySQL Improved) object named $con for database connection using the provided server name, username, password, and database name.

if ($con->connect_error) {: This line checks if the connection to the MySQL server was unsuccessful.

die("Connection failed: " . $con->connect_error);: If the connection fails, the script terminates and outputs an error message.

echo "Connected successfully";: If the connection to the MySQL server is successful, this message is echoed.

$con->close();: This line closes the database connection. It's good practice to close the connection once it's no longer needed.

This PHP program connects the MySQL server and database.

32. Create a table in an existing database

```php
require connect.php;     // Inlude connect.php of Example 31
$sql = "CREATE TABLE IF NOT EXISTS members (
   id INT(6) UNSIGNED AUTO_INCREMENT PRIMARY KEY,
   firstname VARCHAR(30) NOT NULL,
   lastname VARCHAR(30) NOT NULL,
   memo VARCHAR(50),
   set_date TIMESTAMP DEFAULT CURRENT_TIMESTAMP
ON UPDATE CURRENT_TIMESTAMP
)";
if ($con->query($sql) === TRUE) {     // Execute the query
   echo "Table 'members' created successfully";
} else { echo "Error creating table: " . $con->error;  }
$con->close();
?>
```

Explanation:

require connect.php;: Include the "connect.php" of Example 31.

$sql: This variable stores an SQL query for creating a table named "members" if it doesn't already exist.

CREATE TABLE IF NOT EXISTS members: This part of the query creates a table named "members" if it doesn't already exist.

311

(id INT(6) UNSIGNED AUTO_INCREMENT PRIMARY KEY, ...): This defines the columns of the table.

id: An integer column with a maximum length of 6 digits, marked as UNSIGNED (non-negative), set as AUTO_INCREMENT, and designated as the PRIMARY KEY.

firstname, lastname: VARCHAR columns for storing strings up to 30 characters, marked as NOT NULL (meaning they must have a value).

memo: A VARCHAR column for storing strings up to 50 characters.

set_date: A TIMESTAMP column with default and on-update values set to the current timestamp.

$con->query($sql): This line executes the SQL query using the query method of the MySQLi object ($con).

if ($con->query($sql) === TRUE) {: This checks if the query was successful.

echo "Table 'members' created successfully";: If the table creation is successful, this message is echoed.

} else {: If the query fails, this block of code is executed.

echo "Error creating table: " . $con->error;: This line outputs an error message, including details about the error.

$con->close();: This line closes the database connection. It's good practice to close the connection once it's no longer needed.

33. Insert data into a "members" table

Source Code 33

```php
require connect.php;     // Inlude connect.php of Example 31

$firstname = "Ray";      // Sample data to insert

$lastname = "Yao";

$memo = "rayyao@example.com";

// SQL query to insert data into the 'members' table

$sql = "INSERT INTO members (firstname, lastname, memo)
VALUES ('$firstname', '$lastname', '$memo')";

// Execute the query

if ($con->query($sql) === TRUE) {

    echo "New record inserted successfully";

} else {

echo "Error: " . $sql . "<br>" . $con->error;

}

$con->close();

?>
```

Explanation:

require connect.php;

Include the "connect.php" of Example 31.

```php
$firstname = "Ray";

$lastname = "Yao";

$memo = "rayyao@example.com";
```

These lines define sample data for the fields firstname, lastname, and memo that we want to insert into the 'members' table.

```sql
INSERT INTO members (firstname, lastname, memo)
VALUES ('Ray', 'Yao', 'rayyao@example.com')
```

This SQL query inserts a new record into the 'members' table with the provided sample data.

```php
if ($con->query($sql) === TRUE) { ... } else { ... }
```

This block checks if the execution of the SQL query was successful.

If successful, it echoes "New record inserted successfully."

If there's an error, it echoes "Error: " followed by the specific query ($sql) and the error obtained from $con->error.

```php
$con->query($sql)
```

This line executes the SQL query ($sql) on the MySQL database represented by the $con connection object.

```php
$con->close();
```

Closes the connection to the MySQL server.

34. Query the database and fetch data

Source Code 34

```php
require connect.php;     // Inlude connect.php of Example 31

$sql = "SELECT * FROM members";  // Query to fetch data

$result = $con->query($sql);

if ($result) {     // Check if the query was successful

    while ($row = $result->fetch_assoc()) {   // Get data by row

        $firstname = $row["firstname"];     // Access data

        $lastname = $row["lastname"];

        $memo = $row["memo"];

        // Do something with the data (e.g., show it)

        echo "First Name: $firstname, Last Name: $lastname,
Memo: $memo<br>";

    }

    $result->free();     // Free the result set

} else { echo "Error: " . $sql . "<br>" . $con->error; }

$con->close();

?>
```

Explanation:

require connect.php;

Include the "connect.php" of Example 31.

$sql = "SELECT * FROM members";

This line defines an SQL query to select all columns (*) from the table named "members."

$result = $con->query($sql);

Executes the SQL query using the query method of the MySQLi connection object ($con).

The result ($result) is a MySQLi result object or FALSE on failure.

if ($result) { while() {......}......}

The if ($result) block checks if the query was successful. If successful, it enters a loop (while) to fetch each row of the result set. Inside the while loop, data for each row is fetched using $result->fetch_assoc() and displayed (or processed) as needed.

$row = $result->fetch_assoc()

The fetched associative array is assigned to the variable $row.

This allows us to easily access the values of columns in the current row using the column names.

$result->free();

After processing, the result set is freed using $result->free() to release resources. If the query fails, the else block is executed, displaying an error message.

$con->close();

Closes the MySQL connection.

35. Update data in a MySQL table

Source Code 35

```php
require connect.php;    // Inlude connect.php of Example 31

// Define the data we want to update

$nameVariable = "Anna";

$idVariable = 1;

// SQL query to update data

$sql = "UPDATE members SET firstname='$nameVariable'
WHERE id=$idVariable";

// Modify the firstname to 'Anna'

if ($con->query($sql) === TRUE) {

    echo "Record updated successfully";

} else {

echo "Error updating record: " . $con->error;

}

$con->close();    // Close the database connection

?>
```

Explanation:

require connect.php;

Include the "connect.php" of Example 31.

$nameVariable and $idVariable

These variables hold the new value "Anna" for the 'firstname' column ($nameVariable) and the identifier for the record to update ($idVariable).

$sql = "UPDATE members SET firstname='$nameVariable' WHERE id=$idVariable";

This line constructs a SQL query for updating a record.

The UPDATE statement is used to modify existing records in a table. In this case, it updates the 'members' table, setting the 'firstname' column to the value of $nameVariable for the record with an 'id' equal to $idVariable.

SET firstname='$nameVariable'

Modify tne value of the firstname to "Anna".

if ($con->query($sql) === TRUE) { ... } else { ... }

The query() method is used to execute the SQL query on the MySQL database.

If the query is successful ($con->query($sql) returns TRUE), it echoes "Record updated successfully."

If there is an error, it echoes "Error updating record" along with the specific error message ($con->error).

$con->close();

Closes the database connection.

36. Use PHP to sort data from a MySQL table

Source Code 36

```php
require connect.php;     // Inlude connect.php of Example 31

// Retrieve and sort data from the 'members' table

$sql = "SELECT id, firstname, lastname, memo FROM members
ORDER BY lastname, firstname";     // sort the data

$result = $con->query($sql);     // Execute the query

if ($result->num_rows > 0) {

    echo "<table>";

    echo "<tr><th>ID</th><th>First Name</th><th>Last
Name</th><th>Memo</th></tr>";

    while ($row = $result->fetch_assoc()) {

        echo
"<tr><td>".$row["id"]."</td><td>".$row["firstname"]."</td><td>

".$row["lastname"]."</td><td>".$row["memo"]."</td></tr>";

    }     // Output data of each row

    echo "</table>";

} else {  echo "No records found";  }

$con->close();

?>
```

Explanation:

require connect.php;

Include the "connect.php" of Example 31.

$sql = "SELECT id, firstname, lastname, memo FROM members ORDER BY lastname, firstname";

Retrieves data from the 'members' table, including columns id, firstname, lastname, and memo, and sorts the results by the lastname and then firstname.

$con->query($sql);

Executes the SQL query using the MySQLi object $con (which represents the database connection).

if ($result->num_rows > 0) {

Checks if there are rows (records) in the result set.

while ($row = $result->fetch_assoc()) {

Loops through each row in the result set and fetches the data into the associative array $row.

echo "<tr> <td>".$row["id"]."</td> <td>".$row["firstname"]."</td> <td>".$row["lastname"]."</td> <td>".$row["memo"]."</td> </tr>";

Outputs the data for each row within HTML table row tags.

$con->close();

Closes the database connection.

37. Alter table and modify data

Source Code 37

```php
// Inlude connect.php of Example 31

require connect.php;

// Define the SQL statement to modify the table

$sql = "ALTER TABLE members MODIFY firstname CHAR(32) NOT NULL UINQUE";

if ($con->query($sql) === TRUE) {    // Execute the query

    echo "Table altered successfully";

} else { echo "Error altering table: " . $con->error;  }

$con->close();    // Close the MySQL connection

?>
```

Explanation:

require connect.php;

Include the "connect.php" of Example 31.

$sql = "ALTER TABLE members MODIFY firstname CHAR(32) NOT NULL UNIQUE";

This line defines an SQL statement to alter the members table. It modifies the firstname column to be of type CHAR(32), not allowing null values (NOT NULL), and ensures that the values in the firstname column are unique (UNIQUE).

"$sql" is a variable that stores the MySQL query.

ALTER TABLE members

Specifies that we want to alter the members table.

MODIFY firstname CHAR(32) NOT NULL UNIQUE

Specifies the modification for the firstname column. It changes
the data type to CHAR(32), sets the column to disallow null
values (NOT NULL), and adds a constraint to enforce uniqueness
(UNIQUE).

if ($con->query($sql) === TRUE) { ... } else { ... }

This conditional statement checks if the execution of the SQL
query was successful. If successful, it echoes "Table altered
successfully"; otherwise, it echoes an error message along with
the specific error obtained from $con->error.

$con->close();

This line closes the MySQL connection to free up resources.

In summary, this script modifies the structure of the members
table in the database. It changes the firstname column to be of
type CHAR(32), ensures that it cannot contain null values, and
adds a constraint to ensure that the values in this column must
be unique.

38. Delete a row from a MySQL table

Source Code 38

```
// Inlude connect.php of Example 31

require connect.php;

// Define the ID of the row we want to delete

$idVariable = 1;

// Substitute with the ID of the row we want to delete

// SQL query to delete data

$sql = "DELETE FROM members WHERE id=$idVariable";

// Substitute with your table name and column names

if ($con->query($sql) === TRUE) {

    echo "Record deleted successfully";

} else {

echo "Error deleting record: " . $con->error;

}
// Close the database connection

$con->close();

?>
```

Explanation:

require connect.php;

Include the "connect.php" of Example 31.

$idVariable = 1;

This line defines the ID of the row that we want to delete. In this example, it's set to 1. We can substitute this value with the actual ID of the row we want to delete.

$sql = "DELETE FROM members WHERE id=$idVariable";

This line defines an SQL query to delete a record from the members table where the id column matches the value of $idVariable.

DELETE FROM members

Specifies that we want to delete records from the members table.

WHERE id=$idVariable

Specifies the condition for deletion, indicating that only the row with the specified id should be deleted.

if ($con->query($sql) === TRUE) { ... } else { ... }

This conditional statement checks if the execution of the SQL query was successful. If successful, it echoes "Record deleted successfully"; otherwise, it echoes an error message.

$con->close();

This line closes the MySQL connection to free up resources.

Recommended Books by Ray Yao

(**Note:** Each Cheat Sheet contains more than 300 examples,
more than 300 outputs, and more than 300 explanations.)

Paperback Books by Ray Yao

C# Cheat Sheet

C++ Cheat Sheet

Java Cheat Sheet

JavaScript Cheat Sheet

Php MySql Cheat Sheet

Python Cheat Sheet

Html Css Cheat Sheet

MySQL Cheat Sheet

SQL Cheat Sheet

Linux Command Line

C# 100 Q & A

C++ 100 Q & A

Java 100 Q & A

JavaScript 100 Q & A

Php MySql 100 Q & A

Python 100 Q & A

Html Css 100 Q & A

Linux 100 Q & A

C# Examples & Explanations

C++ Examples & Explanations

Java Examples & Explanations

JavaScript Examples & Explanations

Php MySql Examples & Explanations

Python Examples & Explanations

Html Css Examples & Explanations

MySQL Examples & Explanations

R Examples & Explanations

Ruby Examples & Explanations

Visual Basic Examples & Explanations

JQuery Examples & Explanations

Advanced C++ in 8 hours

Advanced Java in 8 hours

AngularJs in 8 hours

C# in 8 hours

C++ in 8 hours

Dart in 8 hours

Django in 8 hours

Erlang in 8 hours

Git Github in 8 hours

Made in the USA
Las Vegas, NV
16 October 2024